Alan Hickey is associate producer on the *Postcards* television series, a welcome change for him after twenty-five years of reporting, writing and producing daily television news. He now gets a kick out of rounding up interesting and entertaining stories about people enjoying themselves all over our great state. Alan lives in Adelaide with his wife, Andrea, and their two children. He also works as a freelance journalist and producer.

Postcards
On the road again

Compiled and edited by Alan Hickey

Written by Alan Hickey, Ron Kandelaars, Keith Conlon and Mike Sexton

from original television scripts

Wakefield Press

Wakefield Press
1 The Parade West
Kent Town
South Australia 5067
www.wakefieldpress.com.au

First published 2002

Copyright © Channel 9 South
Australia Pty Ltd, Adelaide, 2002

Designed by Dean Lahn,
Lahn Stafford Design
Typeset by Clinton Ellicott,
Wakefield Press
Printed and bound by
Hyde Park Press

National Library of Australia
Cataloguing-in-publication entry
Postcards: On the road again.
ISBN 1 86254 597 9.
1. Postcards (Television
program). 2. South Australia –
Guidebooks. I. Hickey, Alan.

Wakefield Press thanks
Fox Creek Wines and
Arts South Australia
for their support.

Popeye the riverboat sails the River Torrens   **Photo by Mick Bradley**

Contents

Introduction

by Keith Conlon

This book records several pilgrimages to parts of South Australia that have long beckoned to me. *Postcards* trips have transported me to the top of Mt Remarkable with its through-the-gum-leaves glimpses of Spencer Gulf and the deep scrubby creases of the lower Flinders Ranges in one direction, and the haze of the Willochra Plain in the other. Memory Cove in Lincoln National Park proved more intimate and melancholy than I had expected as we captured a landscape on film almost identical to the one Captain Matthew Flinders found as he searched hopelessly for eight crewmen drowned there two centuries ago. By contrast, the descent to water level in the great Blue Lake crater was chatty and chirpy.

The good news is that *Postcards* is still thriving after seven years on air. The audience watching the show on television on Sunday afternoons frequently tops 200,000, and on the road we often hear of VHS copies lobbing in lounge rooms from Aberdeen to Zanzibar. The first *Postcards* book was stuffed in some distant Christmas stockings too, many with penned pleas from relatives to 'come and see soon'. And then there's the website containing our weekly scripts and destination details. The whole package is a showcase of South Australia's faces and places. Constant emails from interstate and overseas suggest many use *Postcards* to help plan their South Australian visits.

Postcards: On the road again takes us from the vast and daunting stretches of an outback mail run to the subtle nuances of a walled Japanese garden. The *Postcards* team is unashamedly proud of our home state and we're passionate about showing you the sights and significance of the special places and people that give South Australia its sense of difference.

We hope you return to these gourmet chunks of South Australian experiences often. Delve in for a quick idea for a destination or, when you have time, immerse yourself in tales from our past.

On behalf of the team, thanks again to all the guides, authors, artists, rangers, historians, tourism operators and others who share the passion for our state and help preserve its precious stories. Hope to see you out there soon.

Editor's Note

The secret to *Postcard*'s success is its people – both on and off camera. So my thanks go to the regular crew of Ron Kandelaars, Keith Conlon, Jeff Clayfield, Trevor Griscti, Brenda Richards, David McGraw, Lisa McAskill, Marc Orrock, Brenton Harris and former producer Mike Sexton for their commitment to the program. A big thank you also to Pete Dobré who supplied a wonderful selection of photographs from his magnificent collection; to the Royal Automobile Association of SA for their maps; Gina Inverarity from Wakefield Press for her guidance and efficiency; and all the wonderful people who co-operated with *Postcards* to make the television stories possible and then supplied photos and extra information for the book. A special thank you goes to Debra Kandelaars who, after compiling the first book was always there to generously lend a guiding hand with the second – especially when the going got a bit tough. And of course, thanks to my wonderful wife, Andrea, for her love, encouragement and support, and my delightful children, Declan and Catherine, for their smiles and for leaving Daddy alone while he was working.

Alan Hickey

Meet the Postcards Team

A member of the South Australian Tourism Hall of Fame, *Postcards* is a half-hour tourism lifestyle program produced by a small production team at Adelaide's Channel Nine. *Postcards* goes to air on Sundays at 5.30 pm and, since being launched in 1995, has grown to become the benchmark for travel and lifestyle programs. Its friendly relaxed format is now used in many programs across Australia. The team is committed to producing quality and informative television and that has been rewarded with a loyal and enthusiastic audience. As with all good television shows, *Postcards* has its own website. One of the first South Australian shows to go on-line, www.postcards.sa.com.au is now one of the state's busiest sites containing loads of information about current and past stories.

Adelaide

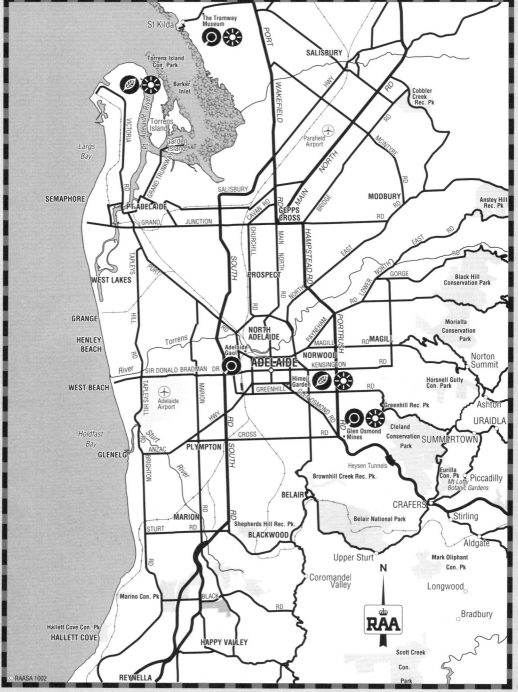

Legend

🍷 Food/Wine   ☀ Walking/Activity   🔍 History/Local Interest   🍃 Nature/Wildlife

St Kilda

The Tramway Museum

SALISBURY

Torrens Island Con. Park

Barker Inlet

Cobbler Creek Rec. Pk

Torrens Island

Parafield Airport

Garden Island

Largs Bay

MODBURY

Anstey Hill Rec. Pk

SEMAPHORE

Salisbury

PT ADELAIDE

GEPPS CROSS

JUNCTION

GRAND

WEST LAKES

PROSPECT

Black Hill Conservation Park

GRANGE

Torrens

NORTH ADELAIDE

Morialta Conservation Park

HENLEY BEACH

Adelaide Gaol

MAGILL

Norton Summit

River

SIR DONALD BRADMAN DR

ADELAIDE

NORWOOD

KENSINGTON

WEST BEACH

Adelaide Airport

Himeji Garden

GREENHILL

Horsnell Gully Con. Pk

Greenhill Rec. Pk

Ashton

Holdfast Bay

CROSS

Glen Osmond Mines

Cleland Conservation Park

URAIDLA

SUMMERTOWN

GLENELG

PLYMPTON

Heysen Tunnels

Eurilla Con. Pk

Piccadilly

ANZAC

Brownhill Creek Rec. Pk.

Mt Lofty Botanic Gardens

MARION

BELAIR

CRAFERS

Shepherds Hill Rec. Pk.

Belair National Park

Stirling

BLACKWOOD

Aldgate

Upper Sturt

Mark Oliphant Con. Pk

N

Marino Con. Pk

Coromandel Valley

Longwood

Bradbury

Hallett Cove Con. Pk

BLACK

HALLETT COVE

RAA

HAPPY VALLEY

Scott Creek Con. Park

REYNELLA

© RAASA 1002

Reverse: Adelaide, the beautiful city in a park

There are few cities in the world quite like Adelaide. With the green backdrop of the Mount Lofty Ranges, it is neatly planned yet manages to retain the charm of an overgrown yet uncrowded provincial city.

Often called a 'city within a park', Colonel William Light's thoughtful planning in 1837 gave the city a wonderful sense of openness. Surrounded by parklands and straddling Lake Torrens, Adelaide is known for its fine heritage architecture and wide, tree-lined avenues like North Terrace. Locals are fond of calling their home the '20-minute city' because for years it was considered possible to drive to most places within that time. The stop-watch may not always have been accurate, but it does sum up a certain unperturbed feel about Adelaide.

Adelaide is home to about a million people and has a reputation as a friendly yet sophisticated place with a variety of restaurants and corner pubs. Add to that its safe, clean beaches and Mediterranean-style climate and you have got a special city worthy of further exploration. And that's what we've done with this collection of *Postcards* stories – they're good examples of the variety of experiences visitors and locals never tire of.

What You'll Find in this Region

• A macabre side of Adelaide history can be found at the Adelaide Gaol where 48 people have been hanged for their dastardly deeds.

• The Port River was originally dubbed 'Port Misery' by the immigrants who disembarked there when Adelaide was still a shanty town. They may have been cheered by the ancestors of the Port River dolphins we're about to meet courtesy of Dr Dolphin.

• We'll take a quiet moment and experience the many different moods of the Adelaide Himeji Garden in the parklands.

• We explore the little known lead and silver mines of Mt Osmond that made Australian mining history.

• A little north of the city is the St Kilda Tramway Museum where we can all experience a form of transport that served Adelaide commuters for half a century.

Tips From the Crew

• Trevor recommends the Marino Rocks Cafe where you'll get great fish and chips and a wonderful coastal view.

• If you haven't been there for a while, Lisa suggests a stroll through the Adelaide Botanic Garden's Bicentennial Conservatory. It's full of lush, tropical plants all housed in the largest greenhouse in the southern hemisphere.

• Jeff says the Sunday morning North Arm Market provides a smorgasbord of fresh fish, fruit and vegetables and homemade produce. Fish is sold straight from the boats and, if you're lucky, you might spot a dolphin looking for a bit of company.

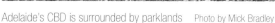
Adelaide's CBD is surrounded by parklands   Photo by Mick Bradley

Want More Information?

SA Visitor and Travel Centre
1300 655 276

Port Adelaide Visitor Centre
(08) 8405 6560

Glenelg Visitor Centre
(08) 8294 5833

Adelaide Passenger Transport
(08) 8210 1000

National Parks and Wildlife SA
(08) 8204 1910

RAA Touring (maps and guides)
(08) 8202 4600

SA Tourism Commission website
www.southaustralia.com

***Postcards* website**
www.postcards.sa.com.au

I Didn't Know That!

- Adelaide was named after Adelheid Amalie Luise Theresa Carolin of Saxe-Meiningen, wife of King William IV.
- The Victoria Square fountain was designed by John Dowie and represents three rivers: the Murray, the Torrens, and the Onkaparinga.

- Adelaide is considered the home of the 'checkside punt', the term coined for a revolutionary football kick developed by Jack Oatey at Sturt Football Club. The kick allows the ball to travel in a curve, enabling players to kick a goal even if they are positioned towards the side of the goal posts. Originally ridiculed by the Victorian football establishment, this skilful kick is now used frequently in the AFL.

- In 1946 Lance Hill built a clothes line out of car parts to help his short wife on washing day. It later became known as the legendary Hills Hoist.
- After bringing the first governor and free settlers to South Australia, HMAS *Buffalo* was later used to transport Canadian convicts to New South Wales and Tasmania.

Adelaide Gaol
with Keith Conlon

I t's a national treasure, but for nearly 150 years no one wanted an invitation to spend any time there. That's because you'd be doing time at the historic Adelaide Gaol. With its carved medieval 'grotesques' or faces, and local limestone walls dating back to 1841, it is Adelaide's oldest major building.

Constructing the gaol in the parklands at Thebarton nearly sent the tiny new South Australian colony broke, which is why Colonial Engineer George Kingston could only afford one grand castle-like tower. He had planned several towers around the walls.

The gaol was used to incarcerate those who fell foul of the law until as recently as 1988 but now we can all experience what life was like behind bars on self-guided and guided tours.

Entering through the giant wooden doors of the front gate, you find yourself in what's called the 'sally port', an arched carriageway through the old two-storey administrative block.

If you were visiting a relative in the early years you'd stand on one side of a barred gate, while on the other side of the grille, with up to eight or nine others, was your loved one. Former 'residents' like Trevor, whose memories are included in the audio tour, reckon it sounded like a Saturday morning cattle auction. Things became a little more civilised in the 1950s when a visitor centre was built.

Take a walk through the 130-year-old, two-storey cell block and you'll find several cells made up to depict daily life through the different eras. It was a model jail in 1841, but it had become a grim embarrassment by the time it closed. Inmates were still sleeping on canvas hammocks until the 1950s, and

while beds and side cupboards had arrived in later years, overcrowding meant that two prisoners would often share a small cell for seventeen hours a day.

The really macabre side of the Adelaide Gaol experience is the gallows. Forty-eight people were executed during the gaol's one-and-a-half centuries of operation. In the 1840s public executions were held on gallows outside the front of the prison. For the last one, in 1854, a couple of thousand people turned up and had a picnic.

After that the hangings were moved inside using portable gallows until 'A Block' was built in 1879. There, an upstairs beam across the central chamber took the rope with a trapdoor waiting below. On the wall there is a list of twenty-one men who, having been found guilty of murder, 'took the drop' here.

The last act of capital punishment was in 1964 when twenty-one-year-old Glen Valance was hanged for shooting his ex-boss on a South East station property. The bodies of all the condemned are buried in the gaol. Simple initials stencilled on the walls are all that mark their graves. Among them is the only woman to be executed in South Australia. Elizabeth Woolcock was found guilty of poisoning her violent husband but despite a mercy plea from the jury she was led to the portable gallows in the yard just after Christmas in 1873 and hanged. Today her tragic story is portrayed in one of the cells of the old three-storey cell block in Yard Two.

These days, for the many visitors, including thousands of school students, all of that is ancient history. But a roam around the cold buildings still gives a sense of what it was like to be a prisoner in this old gaol. Night tours can be arranged and student groups can even stay overnight in an upstairs dormitory. They're all likely to agree with the old saying though – the best thing about Adelaide Gaol is getting out.

18 Gaol Road, Thebarton
South Australia 5031
Tel (08) 8231 4062
Open weekdays 10 am to 4 pm,
Sundays 10 am to 4 pm
(guided tours only)
Night and ghost tours and groups by
appointment

Adelaide
Gaol

Colonial Engineer George Kingston could only afford one grand castle-like tower

Photo by Keith Conlon

Port River Dolphins
with Ron Kandelaars

Cruising the Port River Estuary on the lookout for bottlenose dolphins   Photo by Jeff Clayfield

I t's seven in the morning and the man known as Dr Dolphin is preparing for another departure from the Garden Island Boat Ramp. It's another day at the office for Dr Mike Bossley who's spent fifteen years cruising the reaches of the Port River Estuary in search of bottlenose dolphins.

Within minutes we are joined by a handful of the hundreds of dolphins Mike has come to recognise through his work for the Australian Dolphin Research Foundation. The dolphins have become a full-time job for this semi-retired marine biology lecturer, who says he still enjoys the challenge of learning as much as possible about these unique mammals:

There are probably about twenty or thirty dolphins that are almost permanently here. There'd be another thirty or forty that visit every month or two and then there are some that I see maybe once or twice a year. But there are others that I've only seen once in fifteen years.

While the Port River scenery is stunning, so is Mike's encyclopaedic knowledge of these fascinating creatures. He says there are three main dolphin communities in our waters: those in the Port River, those that cruise our suburban beaches and another group that ventures further up St Vincent's Gulf. But most drop in here at some stage.

Unfortunately, these visits have their dangers. Even though the area is soon to be declared a dolphin sanctuary, Mike says it's time we appreciated the real fragility of the dolphins' attachment to the Port River:

The pollution is causing a problem. Everybody says, if dolphins are so smart how come they live in such a polluted environment? My answer to that is that they probably put their heads out of the water and look around and say, if humans are so smart why are they living in such a polluted environment?

As if on cue, one of Mike's marine acquaintances appears next to the boat, attracted by the familiar pitch of the outboard motor. Mike knows the dolphin by name – Sparkle. He points out the dolphin's distinguishing features – particular scars on her dorsal fin – a legacy of human carelessness and her battles with pollution.

Mike's point is clear – it's in our interest and that of the dolphins to clean up what will always be a key industrial site in Adelaide. He says most of us don't realise how unique the Adelaide dolphin experience really is:

I haven't been able to find another place in the world where so many dolphins are living so close to a million people. We're really fortunate to have them.

When you climb aboard Mike Bossley's dolphin research boat you're about to gain a unique insight into an important marine environment only eighteen kilometres from the city.

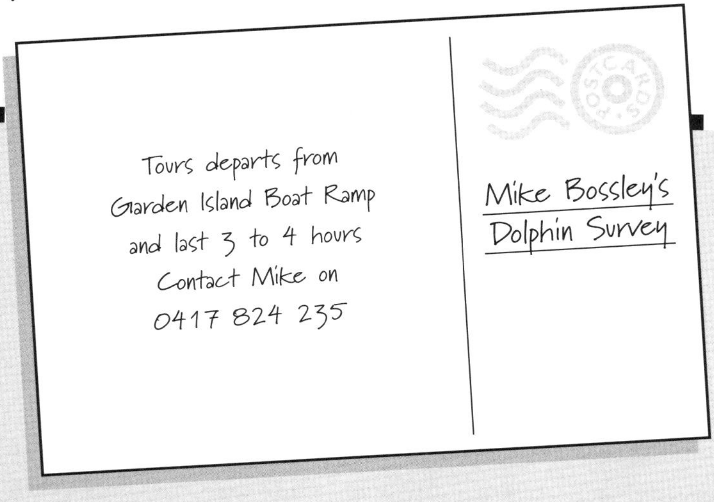

Tours departs from
Garden Island Boat Ramp
and last 3 to 4 hours
Contact Mike on
0417 824 235

Mike Bossley's
Dolphin Survey

The Adelaide Himeji Garden
with Keith Conlon

A stone lantern, a gift from Himeji   Photo by Keith Conlon

A refuge from the city scramble is the best way to describe the Adelaide Himeji Garden in the South Parklands. On South Terrace, where the hills traffic spills into Pulteney Street, the garden is a symbol of the friendship between Adelaide and its Sister City Himeji in southern Japan.

In Japan, Himeji's huge castle garden is revered and, while Adelaide's garden is modest in comparison, it still helps us understand the two classic styles of Japanese garden design. The first is the 'senzui' garden where a small pond should be seen as a vast lake with grand mountains beyond. The second is the 'kare senzui' or dry garden, where rocks and sand suggest sea, land and mountains. Raked, coarse sand represents the oceans while groups of rocks are seen as islands.

Japanese people regard a special place like this garden as an isolated work of art. They believe that by enclosing it with high hedges and walls it can be appreciated all the more because it's separated from the daily grind. The idea of gardens being an artful balance between manufactured and natural beauty goes back more than a thousand

The Adelaide Himeji Garden is a great place for contemplation   Photo by Keith Conlon

years in Japan. As Zen Buddhism grew, garden designers reflected its focus on meditation, and so a very austere and deceptively simple look took hold.

Our Himeji Garden is based on what the experts call a 'stroll garden'. The special language of the garden begins with a temple-like roofed gate. Beneath a bamboo screen and stone lantern is a 'chozubachi' or water bowl. Traditionally it would be placed outside a temple to allow guests to wash before entering.

Upon entering you pass a pond to a waterfall and into the 'mountains', or Nature. The path leads to the teahouse garden with its raked sand and carefully placed boulders.

The tea ceremony originated in the late thirteenth century and aims to create serenity and calm in the hearts of the participants. As in any teahouse in any Japanese garden, there is a stylised 'ido' or well, to provide water for the tea ceremony. In Adelaide's garden, the ido is a carefully carved 'spring' bubbling from a block of ancient-looking stone.

Japan's Himeji castle garden has several sections with teahouses, broad waterfalls and ponds, and exquisitely trained plantings. Visitors go there on a spiritual pilgrimage, taking in its serene beauty and symbolic messages. And while Japan's Himeji castle garden had a five-hundred-year start on the Adelaide version, ours is nevertheless aging gracefully. The Adelaide Himeji Garden is a place for contemplation; it invites you to take a stroll, meditate and sense its many moods.

South Terrace
(near Glen Osmond Road
intersection), Adelaide
South Australia 5000
Tel (08) 8203 7203
www.adelaidecitycouncil.com
Open daily 8 am
to one hour before sunset
Brochures available at the garden

The Adelaide
Himeji Garden

Glen Osmond Mines in the Adelaide Foothills

with Keith Conlon

Glen Osmond today is a fashionable suburb, but 160 years ago it was a rough and tumble area populated by Cornish miners. In 1841 two Cornish men found traces of silver in one of the gullies – a discovery that marked the beginning of mineral mining in Australia.

Take the up-track on the South Eastern Freeway, and turn left into Gill Terrace just metres from the old Tollgate, and you'll find a park framing the entrance to what was Wheal Augusta ('wheal' is Cornish for mine). The mine looks considerably prettier now than it was in

Recovery for an almost bankrupt colony came from mining profits

the 1840s and while the horizontal tunnel behind the iron grille is authentic, Wheal Augusta went nowhere, and soon closed.

It is only one of many tunnels dug throughout the area in search of the valuable silver-lead ore. The miners would dig, pick and blast their way between bluestone blocks and some of them did well enough, with about 2500 tonnes of silver-lead ore extracted during the 1840s.

High above the Wheal Augusta stands a giant stone chimney that was part of one of Australia's first smelters. You can catch a glimpse of it through the trees from Gill Terrace and Sunnyside Road as they snake up towards Mt Osmond. A bluestone flue dug into the steep hill is also still visible, running up from the long-gone smelter in the gully. The round stone chimney used to be whitewashed to serve as a beacon for fishing boats in the gulf.

Thankfully, one of the Glen Osmond gullies further up Sunnyside Drive was considered too steep to build on so was declared a council reserve. It now provides access to

a fascinating link with South Australia's earliest days – two entrances to Wheal Watkins, the biggest of the Mount Osmond mines. As the information boards explain, the main shaft plunged down the equivalent of thirty storeys, or the height of the Santos tower in the city. In just over seven years the miners took out one-thousand tonnes of ore. Much of it was broken down further along the gully by 'pickie-boys' as young as ten. They smashed the rocks with hammers and selected the smeltable pieces for transport.

From the higher entrance above Wheal Watkins Street you get a panoramic view of the Adelaide plains. The lower entrance is down a steep but well-constructed track and it is here that we have organised to meet John Clark, one of the Burnside Historical Society's guides, who takes us along a narrow not-quite-head-high tunnel that drives deep into the mountain. Along the way John points out 'gad holes' – gunpowder-stick sized cylindrical holes laboriously drilled into the bluestone with a gad – a chisel hit with sledgehammers. Half a dozen holes would be drilled and filled – bang! – and they'd start again.

Deep in the hillside, our torches finally reveal the main drive, and in the roof of the tunnel we find a thin strip of clay-white rubble that would have held the sought-after galena ore.

The tour gives a great insight into the way of life for the tough Cornish miners who carved their way into these hills. Their discovery provided the first signs that recovery for the almost bankrupt colony would come from mining. That was certainly the case when copper was later discovered in the mid-north. But it all began in the Adelaide Hills.

The Burnside Historical Society's guides run monthly tours of the Wheal Watkins. Burnside City Council takes the bookings. It is a terrific, time-travelling experience of our underground heritage at the Glen Osmond Mines.

Burnside Historical Society
Tours start at Burnside Council
Chambers on the third Sunday of
each month or groups by appointment
To book call (08) 8366 4224

Glen Osmond
Mine Tours

The Tramway Museum at St Kilda
with Keith Conlon

Adelaide was a tram town for half a century. Trams trundled in every direction from the city to the edge of the suburbs. Those golden days are celebrated at Adelaide's own living, clunking Tramway Museum at St Kilda. Once you arrive at the depot on the edge of the salt flats, there are plenty of trams to catch, with four or five lovingly restored relics rolling up and back on the two-kilometre track to St Kilda Beach every Sunday.

Visiting the Tramway Museum is all about reliving the heyday of a form of public transport that served millions of commuters all round Adelaide. The city's original metro-wide tram system began in 1878 as a horse-drawn service using carriages that came all the way from New York.

Beautifully restored trams run along the St Kilda line every Sunday   Photo by Keith Conlon

The open-sided trams only come out on fine days! · Photo by Keith Conlon

Today the Glenelg tram is the sole survivor of a service that did the city proud until November 1958 when the last tram ran to Cheltenham. At the Tramway Museum, Number 1 is a tram that has a special place for many of the enthusiastic volunteers. Built in Adelaide it was the first to run on the new electric tramway opened in 1909. It still runs back and forth on the tourist track and is often coupled to another tram from the first batch. Old-timers instantly recognise them and remember their nick-names, Bib and Bub.

Many local visitors are surprised to see a Melbourne tram in the collection. But it does have a rightful place in the museum because it's a Holden. It was built in 1924 at Holden's Woodville plant and was a forerunner to Australia's own car.

The day *Postcards* visited the Tramway Museum we took a ride on the Birney – a tram that's certainly been around! Built in Philadelphia with a beautiful timber interior, it first served on the Port Adelaide tram system between Rosewater and Semaphore, then it ran in Geelong in Victoria before being sold to Bendigo Tramway.

You can revive your passenger memories, and the grandkids can take a ride any Sunday. There's also an adventure playground and a fascinating mangrove board walk at the terminus. Allow at least two or three hours to enjoy the fascinating Tramway Museum at St Kilda.

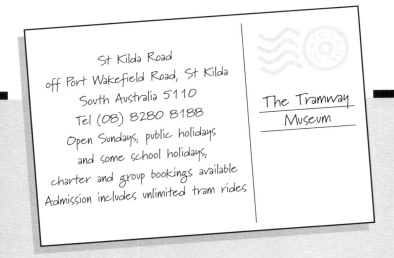

St Kilda Road
off Port Wakefield Road, St Kilda
South Australia 5110
Tel (08) 8280 8188
Open Sundays, public holidays
and some school holidays,
charter and group bookings available
Admission includes unlimited tram rides

The Tramway
Museum

Adelaide Hills

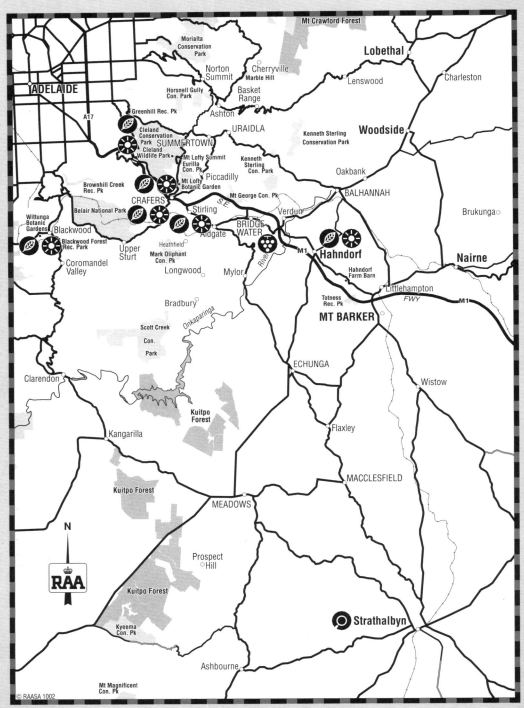

Food/Wine   **Walking/Activity**   **History/Local Interest**   **Nature/Wildlife**

Mt Crawford Forest

Lobethal

Morialta
Conservation
Park

Norton
Summit

Cherryville
Marble Hill

Lenswood

Charleston

ADELAIDE

Horsnell Gully
Con. Park

Basket
Range

Woodside

A17

Greenhill Rec. Pk

Ashton

Cleland
Conservation
Park
Cleland
Wildlife Park

SUMMERTOWN

URAIDLA

Kenneth Sterling
Conservation Park

Mt Lofty Summit
Eurilla
Con. Pk
Mt Lofty
Botanic Garden

Piccadilly

Kenneth
Sterling
Con. Park

Oakbank

Brownhill Creek
Rec. Pk

CRAFERS

Mt George Con. Pk

BALHANNAH

Wittunga
Botanic
Gardens

Belair National Park

Stirling

S.E.

Verdun

Brukunga

Blackwood

Blackwood Forest
Rec. Park

Aldgate

BRIDGE-
WATER

Nairne

Heathfield

M1

Hahndorf

Coromandel
Valley

Upper
Sturt

Mark Oliphant
Con. Pk

Longwood

Mylor

River

Hahndorf
Farm Barn

Littlehampton

FWY

M1

Totness
Rec. Pk

Bradbury

Onkaparinga

MT BARKER

Scott Creek

Con.

Park

ECHUNGA

Wistow

Clarendon

Kangarilla

Kuitpo
Forest

Flaxley

N

MACCLESFIELD

Kuitpo Forest

MEADOWS

RAA

Prospect
Hill

Kuitpo Forest

Strathalbyn

Kyeema
Con. Pk

© RAASA 1002

Ashbourne

Mt Magnificent
Con. Pk

Reverse: Morialta Falls   **Photo by Pete Dobré**

The Adelaide Hills or, more correctly, the Mount Lofty Ranges, stretch from Williamstown in the north to Strathalbyn in the south, and they proved a formidable barrier to the original settlers of the region but eventually gave way to roads, farms, mines, mills and settlements.

Escaping from the city to the Hills has a long tradition. In the early days a little bit of Europe was recreated through the clever use of cooler climate plants among the natives. Adelaide's 'well-to-do' retreated to the Hills to escape the scorching summers of the Adelaide plains. Their legacy is beautiful old houses and gardens – no matter what time of the year.

Today the rolling hills of bush, orchards, market gardens, wineries and farmland are punctuated with charming towns and settlements that offer cool, refreshing retreats from the city. There are plenty of restaurants, wineries, art and craft galleries, music and local produce, while for lovers of the great outdoors there is bushwalking, horse-riding, wildlife, conservation parks and waterfalls galore.

What You'll Find in this Region

- We begin our Hills sojourn at the Bridgewater Mill which played an important role in the 1800s when flour milling was one of South Australia's earliest successful industries.
- Next on the agenda is Cleland Conservation Park, the place to go for a chance to cuddle a koala and learn about our endangered native animals.
- A stroll around an old Adelaide Hills Garden will prompt the question, more English than England?
- Nowhere are South Australia's Scottish links more evident than at Strathalbyn, so we visit the Strathalbyn Courthouse Museum.
- Then, to keep the kids happy, we're off to the German-style village of Hahndorf to see the animals at the Farm Barn.

Tips From the Crew

- Lisa says don't forget to take the kids to see the enchanting Lobethal Christmas Lights – you can catch a return bus from the city if you'd rather not drive.

- When you're off for a drive in the hills, Ron suggests taking your shopping basket and some spare change. Depending on the season, you'll often see roadside signs pointing to a range of fresh produce including strawberries, pears, chestnuts, potatoes, apples, and cherries for sale.

- Keith says head up to Mt Lofty Summit where you'll experience a 360-degree view taking in the city, the coastline and Adelaide Hills valleys and towns.

Gardens in the Hills are a cool, refreshing retreat from the city

Want More Information?

SA Visitor and Travel Centre
1300 655 276

Adelaide Hills Visitor Information Centre
1800 353 323

Adelaide Hills website
www.visitadelaidehills.com.au

Adelaide Hills Circle Link Bus
(08) 8210 1000

National Parks and Wildlife SA
(08) 8204 1910

RAA Touring (maps and guides)
(08) 8202 4600

SA Tourism Commission website
www.southaustralia.com

***Postcards* website**
www.postcards.sa.com.au

I Didn't Know That!

• Early Adelaide Hills residents built their houses from local stringybark, one of only a handful of eucalypts that can be used for construction.

• The Bay to Birdwood Run, a vintage car rally that runs between Adelaide and Birdwood, celebrates the issuing of the first Australian drivers' licences in 1906.
• Former South Australian premier Sir Thomas Playford once lived at Norton Summit and his descendants still live in the area.

• The Great Eastern Steeplechase, held at Oakbank on Easter Monday, is the largest picnic race meeting in the Southern Hemisphere.

Bridgewater Mill
with Keith Conlon

The Old Rumbler still turns

A trip through the Adelaide Hills is not complete without visiting the historic Bridgewater Mill and seeing its spectacular waterwheel known as the Old Rumbler. Built in Scotland and more than eleven metres high, the Old Rumbler's one hundred buckets were once fed by a mill-race – a stone-lined channel that carried the required 30,000 litres of water per minute from the old Bridgewater Mill dam that was tucked away in a secluded valley nearby.

The dam's gone now but the Old Rumbler still turns as it did continuously for a hundred years until 1960. It no longer drives the grinding stones inside to keep the flour mill working – today its slow rotations and splashes are for the benefit of visitors to the flagship of the Adelaide Hills wine region, Petaluma. Winemaker Brian Croser originally used the run-down mill as a place to store his famous sparkling wine:

We built it up to what you see today. There was a hole in the ground; the stone had come out for the mill building itself. And the quarry which surrounded it was the perfect place for storing our wine while it matured in the bottle because the temperature is very even.

Ironically, a tee-totalling Methodist and legendary flour miller named John Dunn, whose produce was famous throughout Australia, built the mill 140 years ago. In fact, the flour from this mill was apparently at the centre of the first 'passing off' case in Australia. According to Brian the flour had such a good reputation for quality that a rival mill, located on Victoria's Bellerine Peninsula near Geelong, copied the brand and sold their flour as Bridgewater Mill flour.

You can dine outside on the deck overlooking Cox Creek

The mill has come a long way since then. Brian bought it in the early eighties for $160,000 on the advice of friend and well-known wine expert Len Evans. Two million dollars later it now boasts an Elizabethan theatre-style interior which is part of the cellar-door and restaurant complex.

Next time you're heading for the Hills, drop in and see the Old Rumbler. Gourmets can dine outside on a raised deck next to the big wheel overlooking Cox Creek and a short stroll after lunch will take you along the nearby Heysen Trail.

Mount Barker Road, Bridgewater
South Australia 5155
Tel (08) 8339 3422
www.bridgewatermill.com.au
Bridgewater Mill restaurant open for
lunch Thursday–Monday
12 pm to 2.30 pm
Cellar door open daily from
10 am to 5 pm
Dinner by appointment

Bridgewater
Mill and
Cellar Door

Cleland Conservation Park
with Keith Conlon

Cleland Conservation Park is a precious green backdrop to the city and a visit offers a chance to get close to some of our native animals. While the whole park covers almost a thousand hectares the wildlife precinct, fenced to keep out feral animals, covers just thirty-five hectares.

You'll probably meet Holly – one of forty koalas in the Cleland colony – forty good reasons why one in three of the park's visitors are overseas tourists. Rangers gently hand the koalas over for a cuddle and a photograph and explain that they are related to wombats and definitely not bears. Koalas eat about a kilogram of gum leaves every day but don't do much else apart from sleep.

You can play hide and seek with the tiny finches and honeyeaters that are native to the Mt Lofty Ranges in the Cleland bush aviary, and the pusher and wheelchair-friendly paths in the wildlife zone take you past inquisitive emus and lazing grey kangaroos, and through a gate into the endangered species area. Here a mini Flinders Ranges rock pile is home to a colony of yellow-footed rock wallabies as Cleland is part of Operation Bounceback, which is ridding the wallabies' natural habitat of foxes and goats and boosting their numbers.

To see nocturnal marsupials like the once plentiful bettongs and bandicoots you can take a guided night-walk when the rabbit-size creatures are best

Feeding time is always popular at Cleland

A tawny frogmouth – one of 100 bird species on exhibit

seen foraging. These walks take you into parts of the hills as they were before land clearing and the unwelcome presence of feral cats and dogs. It's a fascinating night with a strong conservation message.

But Cleland nearly didn't happen – the whole face of the Mt Lofty range was up for sale in the 1920s for housing. Fortunately conservationist Professor J.B. Cleland, who wandered the slopes as a boy, persisted with his campaign about the area being a 'priceless heirloom' until it was bought by the state government in 1945.

Mt Lofty and Mt Bonython are survivors of an ancient mountain range and, according to the Kaurna Aboriginal people of the Adelaide plains, they are Yurridla, the ears of their fallen ancestral being Yurabilla. In Cleland Wildlife Park his story and those of the animals are told on the Yurridla Trail walks.

Almost every day, school groups and a virtual United Nations of visitors settle on the lawns for a wildlife lesson in an outdoor classroom. There are also interactive feeding sessions at set times throughout the day.

A licensed cafe takes care of feeding the humans. And all of this is just nine kilometres as the rosella flies from the GPO. Cleland Wildlife Park is open daily from 9.30 am to 5 pm. If you're travelling from the city take the Crafers exit off the South Eastern Freeway.

Summit Road, Mt Lofty
South Australia 5152
Tel (08) 8339 2444
www.cleland.sa.gov.au
Open daily 9.30 am to 5 pm
(closed Christmas Day)

Cleland
Conservation
Park

Adelaide Hills Gardens
with Mike Keelan

One of the characteristics of the Adelaide Hills is its cooler climate – something the early Europeans seized on, planting European trees and gardens to recreate a 'little bit of home'. So today an autumn drive in the hills can be an unforgettable experience with the brilliant golds and reds of introduced species contrasting with the native grey-green eucalypts.

Epiphany Garden

It stands on top of a hill overlooking the busy South Eastern Freeway but at the Church of the Epiphany at Crafers, the traffic seems a world away, cut off by a peaceful garden retreat. Built in 1878 by Arthur Hardy, the man who built Mt Lofty House, the Church of the Epiphany and the nearby rectory are surrounded by century-old oak trees.

The oaks have flourished in the Adelaide Hills despite nearly being lost in the 1983 Ash Wednesday bushfires. In fact, the flames came within metres of the church and the lower part of the garden was destroyed. You wouldn't know it today with Dianna McGregor's professional make-over

A peaceful pool among the natural rock features

Photo by Dianna McGregor

offering a lesson in good cottage garden design. There's a superbly crafted pool in a natural rock outcrop and plants are in keeping with the plantings of the 1880s like daisies, lillies and hydrangeas.

The Church of Epiphany with its Memorial Gardens is at Epiphany Place at Crafers, off the Summit Road near the Crafers roundabout, and is open to the public seven days a week.

Epiphany Place, Crafers
South Australia 5152
Tel (08) 8339 1274
Open year round

Epiphany
Garden

Mt Lofty Botanic Garden

Mt Lofty Botanic Garden is one of the most visited tourist attractions in the Adelaide Hills. Nestled on the eastern slopes of the Mt Lofty ranges, it's one place I never get tired of visiting – no matter what the season. It offers a great Mediterranean-style view of the beautiful Piccadilly Valley contrasting with the brilliant specimens of cool climate plants thriving amid the Australian eucalypts.

The botanical mix is no accident. It's the brainchild of Noel Lothian who, in 1948, persuaded the Botanic Gardens Board to buy some land in the Adelaide Hills to grow plants from the world's temperate and cold temperate regions, which isn't possible on the Adelaide plains because it's too warm and the soils are alkaline.

Now, just over fifty years on, the Mt Lofty Botanic Garden is a living calendar that heralds in each season with a new burst of life and colour. The centre-piece is a magnificent lake, but my favourite places are the seven gullies dedicated to different plants.

The Mt Lofty Botanic Garden is an inspiration to any 'green thumb'

The magnolia, camellia and rhododendron and rose gullies make the plains-dweller green with envy, and Fern Gully has the richest collection of ferns in Australia. There's also the Bank SA Nature Trail – a well sign-posted one-hour stroll through the stunning native scrub. It's well worth a visit – for an hour or a whole day.

Upper entrance –
Summit Road, Crafers
Lower entrance – best for disabled
– Lampert Road, Piccadilly
South Australia 5151
Tel (08) 8222 9311
Open 8.30 am to 4 pm weekdays,
10 am to 5 pm
weekends and public holidays
Free admission

Mt Lofty
Botanic Garden

Wittunga Botanic Garden

A lesser-known botanic garden in the hills is Wittunga at Blackwood and it's a beauty. This garden is a leafy legacy of one family's passion for plants, especially those native to Australia and South Africa.

It goes back to 1901 and Edwin Ashby who, after clearing the native bush for an orchard, became fascinated with plants from the south-west of Australia and South Africa. Thanks to the generosity of his family, who gave the garden to the state in 1965, the Wittunga Botanic Garden is now a great place to compare the two types of plants. Separated by a lake, on one side are Australian plants – eucalyptus, melaleuca, banksias and grevilleas, and on the other side are the South African ericas and heathland-type plants.

These plants are vital botanical evidence of the great geological phenomena Gondwana – the ancient super continent of which Australia and South Africa were a part. Since the landmass separated, plants that were once neighbours have continued to develop half a world apart. At Wittunga we can see the differences and similarities.

Wittunga Garden contrasts Australian and South African plants

Mind you, you don't have to be a botanist to enjoy Wittunga. It's a great place to have a picnic or spend an afternoon wandering through the plantings. There's even a 'Naming Walk' where our ubiquitous gum trees mingle with bottlebrush and tea trees. The signs that name the trees are useful for suburban gardeners to size up what their nursery purchases could turn into in a few years!

Wittunga Botanic Garden is great for families – the bird life (especially the ducks!) on the lake will keep the kids happy for hours.

Shepherd's Hill Road, Blackwood
South Australia 5051
Open weekdays 8.30 am to 4 pm,
weekends and public holidays
10 am to 5 pm
Guided walks leave from the car park
Call (08) 8222 9311 for details
Free admission

Wittunga
Botanic
Garden

Beechwood Heritage Garden

We often forget that gardens can be a measure of the wealth of a particular period in history. That's well-illustrated with a drive through the leafy streets of many hills towns and villages. A drive through Stirling for example, reveals grand entranceways and gardens beyond that hint of a time when money was no object.

For me, a garden that epitomises that era is Beechwood Heritage Garden at Stirling. Its creator, Francis Hugh Snow, a wealthy merchant who came to Stirling in 1893, spared little expense. He had good contacts in Asia and Europe and he used them to great effect when designing and planting his garden. And although much of what they brought back provides the classic autumn colour found in many South Australian gardens today, in the 1890s Beechwood's liquidambars, Norway maples and various conifers would have looked truly exotic.

The spectacular glasshouse was brought to Australia in kit form

This Victorian-era garden is full of surprises – like the lava-filled rock pool that looks so natural you'd think it was created in a real volcanic eruption, but it's actually man-made. The fabricated rocks were put in blast furnaces, where straw mixed in with the concrete burnt away leaving a very genuine volcanic pitted look.

Later owners carried on the tradition of garden grandeur. I reckon Tom Elder Barr-Smith topped the lot with his classic Victorian-era glasshouse. Originally fabricated in Glasgow it was brought to Australia at the turn of the last century in kit form. It's made of cast iron and is the only one of its type in Australia, possibly the world.

The Beechwood Garden is more fragile than most so is only open for several weeks during spring and autumn. Call the Botanic Gardens for details.

Snows Road, Stirling
South Australia 5155
Call Botanic Gardens
for opening dates on
(08) 8222 9311

Beechwood
Heritage
Garden

Strathalbyn Courthouse Museum
with Lisa McAskill

The old dry-stone walls which criss-cross the fields near Strathalbyn and Macclesfield serve as a constant reminder of the history of this picturesque part of the Adelaide Hills. The people who built them were determined to leave their mark and they also wanted a permanent reminder of where they'd come from. A visit to one of the Adelaide Hills' most interesting museums located in the Old Courthouse and Police Station at Strathalbyn is a great way to learn about the efforts of these early pioneers.

The Old Courthouse Museum gives a real insight into the lives of the early pioneers

Wealthy pastoralist William Rankine arrived in Strathalbyn in 1839 and was followed by the first Scottish pioneers. The Rankines named the town: 'strath' is Scots for a valley with a river, and 'albyn' is for the Albion mines in Scotland. The Angas River remains a feature of this classified Heritage Town. Large areas of parkland on both sides of the Angas create a delightful garden in the centre of town.

Maintaining the Old Courthouse Museum is a labour of love for artist and historian Nancy Gemmell. In the old police station, built in 1858, you can see what it would have been like to be the local trooper in charge of the well-preserved cells and outside stables.

The museum gives a real insight into the social attitudes of the early pioneers. The old bathing notices for the Angas River show they certainly believed in covering up. According to Nancy, it had more to do with ultra conservatism than ultra violet:

We have the original notices they used to stick on the trees by the river. The rules were pretty strict – women weren't allowed to go down to the river when men were there. And for a very long time the girls couldn't swim at all.

The Old Courthouse Museum is just one of the thirty or so buildings in Strathalbyn that are of historic interest. You'll find it in Rankine Street, Strathalbyn, and it's open on weekends, public and school holidays.

1 Rankine Street, Strathalbyn
South Australia 5255
Tel (08) 8536 3212
Open 2 pm to 5 pm weekends,
public and school holidays

Old
Courthouse
Museum

Hahndorf Farm Barn
with Mark Bickley

An opportunity for city kids to get their hands dirty

Photo by Malcolm Farmer

My wife, Tanya, and I loaded the Bickley tribe in the car one weekend and headed for the hills in search of something a little different. We found it just up the road from Hahndorf at the Farm Barn – a working farm with an emphasis on hands-on experience. It's a great place for city kids to sample life on the land.

The Bickley mob didn't need much encouragement. Within minutes they had set about rounding up some sheep. According to Malcolm Farmer (yes, that is his real name!), who runs the Hahndorf Farm Barn with his wife, Marie, son Michael and *his* wife, Kate, that's what it's all about – allowing kids of all ages to experience nature at very close quarters:

We've had kids come here who won't touch the animals. They drop a baby chicken because they say it's going to scratch them. But half an hour later they're playing with everything and it's a joy to see. They learn that animals won't hurt them.

That sort of gently, gently approach certainly wasn't needed with our kids. After helping to feed the new spring lambs it was into the rabbit enclosure where Tash grabbed a bunny of her own.

The highlight of the day was Daisy the Cow

Photo by Malcolm Farmer

The day we were there, a group of overseas travel agents were watching Mike's regular shearing demonstration. Mike says that for many people, this is the only time they get a chance to see a real sheep being shorn.

The kids were intrigued with the shearing for a while but their attention soon turned to the guinea pig enclosure, then the honey bee display, then the goats and alpacas. But the highlight of the day was Daisy the cow. She's a Jersey with an enormous amount of patience – demonstrated while letting the Bickley clan have a go at milking. For a Port Pirie lad like me, milk is something that comes from a carton but under Michael's expert tutelage, I was soon producing results.

If you're looking for something to do with the family you won't find much better than watching them play with the animals at the Hahndorf Farm Barn. It's open daily and is on the Mt Barker Road at Hahndorf next to the historic Nixons Mill.

Mt Barker Road, Hahndorf
South Australia 5245
Tel (08) 8388 7289
Open daily 9 am to 5 pm
(except Christmas and Boxing Day)

Hahndorf
Farm Barn

Fleurieu Peninsula

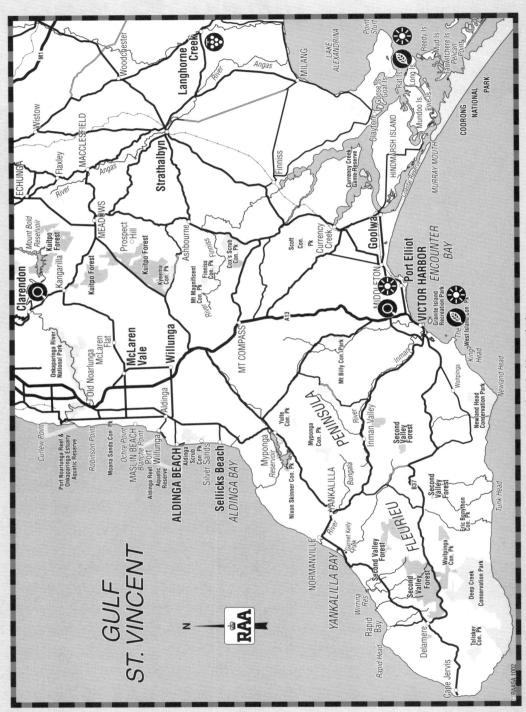

Food/Wine **Walking/Activity** **History/Local Interest** **Nature/Wildlife**

GULF
ST. VINCENT

Clarendon

ECHUNGA
Wistow
Flaxley
MACCLESFIELD
Strathalbyn
Langhorne Creek
Woodchester
MILANG
LAKE ALEXANDRINA
Point Sturt
Reedy Is.
Mud Is.
Rat Is.
Long Is.
Goose Is.
Dove Is.
Mundoo Is.
Ewe Is.
Pelican Point
COORONG NATIONAL PARK

River Angas
River Angas
Angas

MEADOWS
Prospect Hill
Ashbourne
Finniss

Mount Bold Reservoir
Kuitpo Forest
Kangarilla
Kuitpo Forest
Kuitpo Forest
Kyeema Con. Pk
Mt Magnificent Con. Pk
Finniss Con. Pk
Finniss
Cox's Scrub Con. Pk
Scott Con. Pk
Currency Creek
Currency Creek Game Reserve
Clayton
HINDMARSH ISLAND
MURRAY MOUTH

Goolwa
MIDDLETON
Port Elliot
VICTOR HARBOR
ENCOUNTER BAY

Onkaparinga River National Park
McLaren Flat
McLaren Vale
Willunga
MT COMPASS
A13
Mt Billy Con. Park
Inman
Granite Island Recreation Park
The
West Island Con. Pk
King Head

Old Noarlunga
Aldinga
Inman Valley
Waitpinga

Curlew Point
Port Noarlunga Reef & Onkaparinga Estuary Aquatic Reserve
Robinson Point
Ochre Point
Blanche Point
Moana Sands Con. Pk
Aldinga Reef Port Willunga Aquatic Reserve
MASLIN BEACH
Aldinga Scrub Con. Pk
Silver Sands
ALDINGA BEACH
Sellicks Beach
ALDINGA BAY

Myponga Reservoir
PENINSULA
Yulte Con. Pk
Myponga Con. Pk
River
Inman Valley
Second Valley Forest
Newland Head Conservation Park
Newland Head

Myponga
Nixon Skinner Con. Pk
YANKALILLA
Bungala
Second Valley Forest
B37
Eric Bonython Con. Pk
Tunk Head

NORMANVILLE
River
Yarnet Kelly Park
FLEURIEU
Second Valley Forest
Second Valley Forest
Waitpinga Con. Pk
Deep Creek Conservation Park

YANKALILLA BAY
Wirrina Res.
Rapid Bay
Rapid Head
Delamere
Talisker Con. Pk
Cape Jervis

N
RAA

Reverse: Second Valley, Fleurieu Peninsula **Photo by Pete Dobré**

Base map and data supplied courtesy of the RAA of SA Inc. and reproduced with permission

© RAASA 1002

The Fleurieu Peninsula lies to the south of the Mount Lofty Ranges and is a region of contrasting landscapes – the rolling hills and valleys of the ranges, the fertile flat plains that stretch towards Lake Alexandrina, and the ruggedness of the Cape Jervis and Deep Creek coastline. There are also beaches for all tastes ranging from roaring surf to wide, sandy, sheltered bays.

Touring the Fleurieu is easy either for the day or an extended stay. Try entering via the back door – the historic town of Clarendon. The region boasts sixty cellar-door wineries, many cafes and restaurants, and roadside stalls selling local produce are scattered across the peninsula.

The unofficial Fleurieu capital is Victor Harbor which, along with the other coastal towns, explodes with holiday-makers during summer. The annual return of southern right whales to the waters around Encounter Bay is an added attraction.

These stories scarcely scratch the surface of what's on offer so take the easy trip south soon and find out for yourself just how accessible the Fleurieu Peninsula really is.

What You'll Find in this Region

- Start your exploration of the Fleurieu Peninsula at Clarendon, a beautifully preserved town with plenty to see and do.
- No visit to Victor Harbor is complete without a trip across to Granite Island – but an after-dark trip reveals a whole new attraction.
- Next stop is Langhorne Creek, one of Australia's oldest wine districts and a region that enjoys a good flood.
- A trip on the *SteamRanger* is a must for all first-time visitors to the Fleurieu . . . and second-timers and third . . .
- Our Fleurieu tour finishes with a fascinating cruise around the Islands at the End of the Murray that witnessed the boom times of the riverboat era.

Tips From the Crew

- Trevor recommends a walk down to Hindmarsh Falls in winter. At the bottom of a number of stairs you'll discover a spectacular waterfall. Watch your step on the way!

- Ron suggests heading off to Deep Creek Conservation Park at sunset. You'll find yourself in the company of mobs of large, grey kangaroos.
- Lisa recommends a day trip wandering through Strathalbyn and Willunga's antique and bric-a-brac shops.

- Keith says next time you're heading towards Victor Harbor, take a detour and head along the Mount Compass Produce Trail, where you'll be greeted with a smorgasbord of terrific local produce.

Ingallala Falls   Photo by Pete Dobré

Want More Information?

SA Visitor and Travel Centre
1300 655 276

Fleurieu Peninsula website
www.fleurieupeninsula.com.au

McLaren Vale and Fleurieu Visitor Centre
(08) 8323 9944

Victor Harbor Information Centre
(08) 8552 5738

Goolwa Information Centre
(08) 8555 1144

National Parks and Wildlife SA
(08) 8552 3677

RAA Touring (maps and guides)
(08) 8202 4600

SA Tourism Commission website
www.southaustralia.com.au

***Postcards* website**
www.postcards.sa.com.au

I Didn't Know That!

• Our state's first industry was a whaling station, set up at Encounter Bay in 1837.

• It takes about sixty walking days to complete the entire length of the 1500 kilometre Heysen Trail which begins at Cape Jervis and ends in the Flinders Ranges.

• The seventeen kilometre stretch of water separating the mainland from Kangaroo Island is called Backstairs Passage and was named by Captain Matthew Flinders in 1802.

Clarendon

with Keith Conlon

Early spring in Clarendon   Photo by Keith Conlon

The pretty town of Clarendon, snug in an Onkaparinga River valley, was once an isolated village but now it's the delightful gateway to the Fleurieu Peninsula. In its earliest days, Clarendon's villagers had to walk several kilometres up Chandler's Hill and all the way down to O'Halloran Hill to catch the stagecoach to Adelaide. These days, the city is only a half-hour away via Main South Road.

Clarendon's pioneering days began in 1846, and a stroll along the main street reveals many well-preserved links with the town's founders Richard and Jeremiah Morphett. They were related to the famous John Morphett of Cummins House and, of course, Morphettville Racecourse. Their cousin George held land up the steep rise of the valley, and he offered a piece of it to any Christian denomination who cared to build on it. So as early as 1851, the Wesley Methodists took up his offer and built the tiny Mt Zion Church. Within a decade or so, teetotallers were looking down from its doors upon the boozers below at the Royal Oak Hotel.

A number of the main street buildings date back to the 1850s gold rush days. There was a boot-maker and saddler, a butcher and blacksmith. And Bible Christians used to come to town from their dairies and orchards to a simple but beautiful house of worship built in 1854 on the main road. It now houses the National Trust Museum, which opens by appointment.

The Onkaparinga River takes a sharp left turn under old sedimentary cliffs beside Clarendon where a causeway footpath leads to a picnic ground inside the bend – just the spot to eat a legendary Clarendon pastie from the nearby bakery. The picnic park is where the Ngarrindjeri people held corroborees on their way to Adelaide to collect blankets for the winter ('onkaparinga' means 'women's river' in Kaurna Aboriginal stories).

There's a pretty, arched road bridge across the river – the second built on the site. The original was made of laminated redgum in 1858, and the concrete version is early twentieth-century – less romantic, but constructed for a thousand pounds under the original £3000 budget.

Clarendon has strong links with the wine industry. The first vines of the Old Clarendon Winery were cultivated in the 1840s and within a few years they covered the steep hillside above the Onkaparinga. They were removed, but now new plantings reproduce the old scene. An early parliamentarian, Edward Peake, built a steep and triple-gabled winery on the hill, and the 1850s building is now a popular accommodation centre.

Clarendon is located in the Adelaide Hills just before they meld into McLaren Vale and the Fleurieu Peninsula, so it's easy to visit on a day trip. You're sure to love this southern hills hamlet and want to linger a while longer. There's a great walking guide available from the general store.

66 Grants Gully Road, Clarendon
South Australia 5157
Tel (08) 8383 6020

Walking guides available from
Clarendon
General
Store

Granite Island Penguin Tour
with Lisa McAskill

As the horse-drawn tram takes the last day-time visitors back across the causeway to Victor Harbor, the stars of Granite Island's night-time show prepare for their performance.

Granite Island is home to about 1800 penguins and, to protect the tiny birds, the island is closed to public access after sunset. The only way to see their moonlight activities is on a Granite Island Penguin Tour.

My nocturnal island experience began at the Penguin, Marine and Environmental Centre. Suzanne Minards was our guide and she explained that the little penguin, sometimes known as the fairy penguin, is the world's smallest penguin species, growing to about thirty-five centimetres and weighing about one kilogram. Before we set out Suzanne told us that the birds have strict right of way – so if they happened to cross our path during the tour we should stop and let them pass. She also reminded us that we were about to enter their environment so it was important that we disturb them as little as possible:

Penguins' eyes are six times more sensitive than humans' so we use torches with special red lenses that don't bother them too much.

The penguins nest in burrows in the craggy hills and cliffs where the chicks spend the days waiting for their parents to return at dusk with dinner. The cries of hundreds of hungry chicks encourage their parents as they emerge cautiously from the sea. Eventually one bold bird steps forward and it becomes something of a race as the penguins hurry through their boulders and into the burrows.

Mature penguins can go as far as ten kilometres offshore and swim between thirty and fifty kilometres a day in search of fish and squid. Some have been known to swim as far as one hundred kilometres in a day. No wonder they appear a little tired when they return to the rocky shores of Granite Island. Suzanne explains that all that feeding also takes its toll:

When the penguins have had a really big feed it takes them about eight hours to digest the food. They then rest, sometimes for as long as twenty hours, which we call a PDO or a penguin day off.

The fairy penguin is the world's smallest penguin species

There's safety in numbers for penguins and, after dark, Granite Island is almost over-run with the comical little waddlers on their evening parade. The show they put on is certainly worth catching. The evening tours conducted by experienced and informed guides take up to two hours and it's all part of the Granite Island Nature Park that includes an aquarium, cruises, bistro, kiosk and gift shop.

Granite Island, Victor Harbor
South Australia 5211
Tel (08) 8552 7555
email granite@chariot.net.au
website www.graniteisland.com.au
Open daily 10 am to sunset,
penguin tours begin at sunset,
bookings essential

Granite Island
Nature Park

The Causeway, Victor Harbor
South Australia 5211
Tel (08) 8552 5738
email vhtic@granite.net.au
website www.tourismvictorharbor.com.au
Open daily 9 am to 5 pm

Victor Harbor
Visitor
Information
Centre

Langhorne Creek
with Keith Conlon

The Langhorne Creek region relies on a good flood to improve its wine   Photy by Nigel Parsons

Langhorne Creek is one of the most fascinating but least known of Australia's wine regions. To understand the regions' grapevine-growing success, we need to start high in the Mt Lofty Ranges. As the water flows off the hills down to the plains that stretch towards Lake Alexandrina, it carries a load of silt and nutrients that add to the already fertile, alluvial loam on the flats. This is what has made Langhorne Creek a grape grower's heaven today.

A search for a Langhorne Creek will prove fruitless as one simply doesn't exist. When Alfred Langhorne was overlanding cattle from Sydney and holding them here in 1841, the place where he crossed the Bremer River was referred to as Langhorne's Crossing, so the name Langhorne Creek evolved. We found the Bremer to be a deep, dry river-bed lined with stocky river red gums. It was hard to imagine that the river bursts its banks and floods regularly.

The Bridge Hotel, built before the rambling town, would have made a quid or two back then from the optimistic thousands heading for the Victorian goldfields in the 1850s.

Today you can sample the flavour of the old town at the Bremer Restaurant near the bridge. A gallery of photographs portray a rustic village where it paid to keep a boat handy if you were wanting to slip down to the pub when the flood was on. Further down the main road is the Oddfellows Hall. It still stands after more than 130 years service as a concert hall, make-shift church, doctor's rooms and silent movie venue.

The waiting game – good wine can't be rushed

Photo by Nigel Parsons

The Langhorne Creek region is one of the nation's oldest wine districts and now the fastest growing. The old and new come together at the Lake Breeze Winery. The Follett family built a homestead at the end of a winding track through the vines here in the 1850s and in the last decade they've lifted the Lake Breeze wine label to lofty heights. Winemaker Greg Follett works with his two brothers and father, and their partners, so when you call in on the renovated old implement-shed-turned-cellar-door it is definitely a family affair.

The family feeling is just as strong up the road at Bremerton Winery. In 1985 the Willsons bought an alfalfa farm and planted grapes. They also restored the 1860s homestead built for William Hill, who probably ran coaches and freight carts because his two-storey stone stable had sixteen horse bays. Now the stable is the cellar door for Rebecca Willson's highly regarded estate wines. Her sister Lucy and mother and father, Mignonne and Craig, make up the team.

The first bloke to really catch on to the potential of the rich flood plain along the Bremer was the legendary Frank Potts. He came out on the *Buffalo* in 1836. After a pioneering stint at American River on Kangaroo Island, he was on his way to becoming ferry-master at Wellington on the Murray. He saw these fertile flood plains and big river red gums and, in 1850, bought 120 acres. Within ten years the first vines were in and five generations later, the Potts family is still picking grapes.

Inside Frank's Bleasdale Winery, the giant red gum press he built is still occasionally swung into action. Great-great grandson, Michael Potts, is one of the winemakers and the day we were there he gave the okay to let the massive two-and-a-half-ton timber beam down on the 110th vintage. The family's photographic collection also celebrates the many talents of Frank Potts. In the 1870s he built five paddle-steamers for the booming Murray River trade.

The Langhorne region isn't only good for growing grapes – it's also the home of the connoisseur's condiment – horseradish. These days F.C. Newman Horseradish is a South Australian household name. It was originally part of the famous Newman's Nursery business at Tea Tree Gully. About seventeen years ago the owners Brian Meakin and his father, moved the farm to the deep rich soil next to the Bremer River. It was a wise move as now they churn out more than 4000 jars a week.

There's no doubt Langhorne Creek is a magical moment on the Fleurieu Peninsula. Like each of our wine regions, it has its own distinctive feel and look. The flat river delta is dissected by the meandering Bremer River and studded with stout, ancient river red gums and, as the locals say, they won't be able to keep it a secret forever.

PO Box 78, Langhorne Creek
South Australia 5255
Tel (08) 8537 3362
email info@langhornewine.com.au
website www.langhornewine.com.au
Guide brochures available at most
Langhorne Creek shops
and businesses

Langhorne
Creek
Wine Industry
Council

The Railway Station
South Terrace, Strathalbyn
South Australia 5255
Tel (08) 8536 3212
Open Monday to Friday
9 am to 5 pm,
Saturday and Sunday 10 am to 4 pm

Strathalbyn
Visitor
Information
Centre

SteamRanger's Cockle Train
with Lisa McAskill

The story of *SteamRanger* begins in a shed at the Mt Barker Railway Station where Ron Williams and his offsider John Davidson work on an old F251 – a steam-driven locomotive which once operated on Adelaide's suburban network.

Built in 1922 at Gawler, it operated until the 1960s and for a time was rusting away in a shopping centre car park. That is until *SteamRanger*'s volunteer army got their hands on it. Every day they pamper and polish steel, brass and cast iron so that one day the trains can be fired up to do what they do best. Based in Mt Barker in the Adelaide Hills, *SteamRanger* runs unforgettable half and full day rail excursions to Strathalbyn and Victor Harbor on the Fleurieu Peninsula.

The day we climbed aboard we were reliving the days when Loco Rx207, built in 1913, rolled along the track. After five years of restoration it's back in service as the Cockle Train – one of the trains the *SteamRanger* enthusiasts run between the historic port of Goolwa and Victor Harbor.

The latest addition to the fleet rattles along at a comfortable fifty kilometres per hour, burning up about a third of a tonne of coal as it flies through the twenty-six level crossings on the journey.

For the children from a nearby school it's a big day out and so too for volunteer guard Pete Blake who oversees the train's departure from Port Elliot. The railway to this point was Australia's first iron rail public line and was built to take River Murray trade from Goolwa to what was then the nearest sea port, as Pete explains:

The line began as a horse-drawn tram between Goolwa and Port Elliot in 1854. The horses pulled a four-wheel truck until it was established that Port Elliot wasn't a very safe port. Following a number of shipwrecks the line was extended to Victor Harbor.

And that's where we were heading as we steamed over Watson's Gap where an arched reinforced concrete bridge has replaced the original 1860s timber structure. Then it was onto the 1907 five span concrete bridge over the Hindmarsh River.

The classic coastal scenery slips by and we relive what thousands of commuters and tourists have experienced in these carriages on this famous coastal line. The Cockle Train is just another part of a rolling piece of history that makes a return trip from Goolwa to Victor every Sunday and public holiday.

The Cockle Train is only steam-powered on some Sundays and during school holidays. At other times it's a rail car, so it pays to check if you want a steam experience.

Cockle Train runs between Goolwa Wharf and Victor Harbor station

The Cockle Train

Dutton Road, Mt Barker
South Australia 5251
Tel (08) 8391 1223
Departure times vary
For details and a full timetable phone
(08) 8231 4366

SteamRanger Booking Service
Tel (08) 8231 4366

SteamRanger Depot

The Cockle Train is a classic Fleurieu experience

The Islands at the End of the Murray
with Keith Conlon

The *Wetlands Explorer* lands at a Coorong beach

The Islands at the End of the Murray are a secret shared only by the Goolwa boaties – there is Goose Island, Goat Island, Mundoo and more. The islands hinder the great river's opening to the southern ocean and create a paradise for many species of birds.

As the morning cloud cleared to reveal a sparkling blue sky, the *Postcards* team joined passengers on the boat *Wetlands Explorer* as it departed from the biggest and best-known of the island group, Hindmarsh Island. We slid past some of the 600 or so yachts and cruisers at the mooring jetties and waved to the morning coffee crowd at Rankine's Landing. The tavern is operated by Peter Rankine, a descendent of Dr Rankine of Strathalbyn who took up the first stock grazing lease there back in 1847. A few years later Captain Cadell sailed a paddle-wheeler from Sydney, and headed upstream to pioneer the riverboat era. Goolwa began to live the dream of becoming the New Orleans of the south.

Following Cadell's path we soon left Goolwa behind and it wasn't long before our knowledgeable guide and skipper Peter Summerton was pointing out some limestone cliffs. They date to a geological era when the Murray was a massive waterway, cutting a ditch and pouring into the sea somewhere south of Kangaroo Island.

Today the low islands like Goose and Rat are difficult to distinguish from reeds and shallows and Peter says the Murray in this area used to look a lot different:

The water used to run crystal clear and twenty-feet deep as fresh water came down from the Snowy Mountains. At other times it would run the other way as a flush of saltwater rushed in through the Murray mouth from the ocean. That, of course, was before the barrages.

Fifteen kilometres upstream from Goolwa the *Wetlands Explorer* moors on the banks of a well hidden cattle station on Mundoo Island. Paddle steamers once used the old jetty here to pick up cargo and drop supplies. One of them, the PS *Wilcannia* was dismantled and some of the remnants were used to construct buildings and stockyards.

From here we hopped aboard a mini-bus for a tour of an unlikely cattle station that has islands for paddocks. Fourth generation Mundoo Island owner, Colin Grundy, and his wife, Sally, welcome visitors to their island farm and, as Colin drives and checks their one thousand or so Angas cattle, Sally tells amazing tales of the pioneering days. She points out the remnants of a jetty and the town built in the 1930s to house the workers and their families while they built the barrages.

After a quick barbecue lunch at the old blacksmith shop back at Mundoo Island Landing we climb aboard the *Wetlands Explorer* for another rare experience. At one end of the 1.6-kilometre-long Tauwitcherie Barrage is a hand-operated lock – and I soon found out that I was to play a part in us getting through to the briny Coorong on the other side. With a hefty haul on the winch handle, the wooden roadway across the lock swings aside. With a little more muscle-power the lock gates slide back into the concrete walls. Peter gave me the thumbs-up to open the valves and after the water slowly dropped a couple of metres, we emerged on the salt water side of the fragile Coorong.

The Coorong is home to thousands of water birds – pelicans, waders like the long-legged stilts and avocets with their upturned beaks, and plump migratory birds feeding up for their late autumn flight to Siberia. They all contribute to the sense of wilderness that inspired Colin Thiele's *Storm Boy*.

Peter took us ashore to climb giant sand hills and take in the views of the lakes and lands that sustained the eighteen tribes of the Ngarrindjeri people. We saw middens – feasting areas – that are piled so high their age is counted in thousands of years. This area supported a number of semi-permanent settlements of Ngarrindjeri people for over six thousand years.

At the end of our journey we reached the mouth of the mighty Murray River. Except for a shallow tidal flow inwards, the mouth of the enormous Murray Darling river system is pitifully closed. Hardly a skerrick of river water is left to run into the Southern Ocean.

The Coorong is home to amazingly varied bird life – from pelicans to emus

Despite the sorry sight, the serenity of the islands, wildlife and the natural beauty of the Coorong endure and a cruise on the *Wetlands Explorer* received a unanimous recommendation from our fellow passengers.

Sally and Colin Grundy run separate one-hour tours of their cattle station on the islands. The tour crosses the barrages and visits Mundoo and Ewe Islands exploring their history and natural attractions including the spectacular birdlife and Coorong. It begins and ends with a free pick-up service on Hindmarsh Island.

Peter and Jo Summerton
The Marina, Hindmarsh Island
South Australia 5214
Tel (08) 8555 1133
email peternjo@esc.net.au
website www.coorongtours.com

Coorong
Cruises

Sally and Colin Grundy
Mundoo Island, via Goolwa
South Australia 5214
Tel (08) 8555 2242
Mob 0418 843 299
email mundoopc@granite.net.au

Mundoo Island
and Coorong
Tours

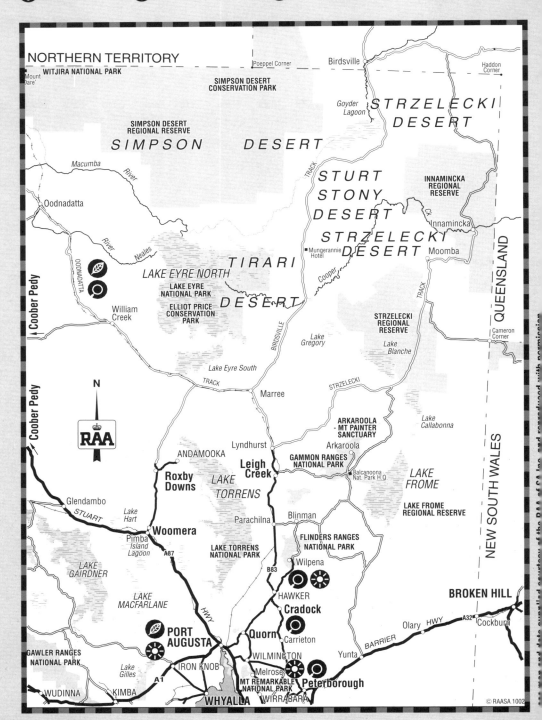

Food/Wine　　Walking/Activity　　History/Local Interest　　Nature/Wildlife

NORTHERN TERRITORY

Mount Dare'

WITJIRA NATIONAL PARK

Poeppel Corner

Birdsville

Haddon Corner

SIMPSON DESERT CONSERVATION PARK

STRZELECKI DESERT

Goyder Lagoon

SIMPSON DESERT REGIONAL RESERVE

SIMPSON DESERT

STURT STONY DESERT

INNAMINCKA REGIONAL RESERVE

Macumba River

Innamincka

STRZELECKI DESERT

Moomba

Oodnadatta

Neales River

River

OODNADATTA

Mungerannie Hotel

Cooper

QUEENSLAND

Coober Pedy

TIRARI

William Creek

LAKE EYRE NORTH

LAKE EYRE NATIONAL PARK

ELLIOT PRICE CONSERVATION PARK

DESERT

STRZELECKI REGIONAL RESERVE

Cameron Corner

Lake Gregory

Lake Blanche

BIRDSVILLE

Lake Eyre South

TRACK

Marree

STRZELECKI

N

RAA

Coober Pedy

Glendambo

Lake Callabonna

ARKAROOLA - MT PAINTER SANCTUARY

Lyndhurst

Arkaroola

ANDAMOOKA

Leigh Creek

GAMMON RANGES NATIONAL PARK

Balcanoona Nat. Park H.Q.

LAKE FROME

Roxby Downs

LAKE TORRENS

STUART

Lake Hart

Woomera

Parachilna

Blinman

LAKE FROME REGIONAL RESERVE

Pimba

A87

Island Lagoon

LAKE TORRENS NATIONAL PARK

FLINDERS RANGES NATIONAL PARK

NEW SOUTH WALES

LAKE GAIRDNER

LAKE MACFARLANE

B83

Wilpena

HWY

HAWKER

BROKEN HILL

GAWLER RANGES NATIONAL PARK

PORT AUGUSTA

Cradock

Quorn

Carrieton

Olary HWY

A32

Cockburn

Lake Gilles

IRON KNOB

WILMINGTON

Yunta

BARRIER

Lake Gilles

A1

Melrose

MT REMARKABLE NATIONAL PARK

Peterborough

WUDINNA

KIMBA

WHYALLA

WIRRABARA

© RAASA 1002

Reverse: Arkaba Woolshed, Flinders Ranges　　**Photo by Pete Dobré**

The Flinders Ranges and Outback are distinctly South Australian. The vastness of the country up north is almost beyond comprehension. Stretching to the west, north and east, the endless expanse of heat-shimmering deserts, dunes, gibber country and ranges beckon to the adventurous traveller.

Thanks to the increasing popularity of four-wheel-drive vehicles more people are experiencing the South Australian Flinders Ranges and Outback. The Simpson Desert, the world's largest parallel dune system, the bizarre Mars-like terrain of Coober Pedy, and the magic of Lake Eyre are now more accessible than ever before. *Postcards* did it the easy way on the Outback Mail Run – from the Dingo Fence to the old Ghan Line.

The jagged peaks of the Flinders Ranges have inspired artists like Sir Hans Heysen, who talked of the Flinders as 'the bones of nature laid bare'. For most of us the gateway to the outback is Port Augusta where a visit to the award-winning Wadlata Outback Centre and the Arid Lands Botanic Garden give a glimpse of what lies ahead. The southern Flinders are even closer with Mt Remarkable and the pretty town of Melrose at its base – only a few hours drive from the city.

What You'll Find in this Region

- The Arid Lands Botanic Garden displays the tough flora that covers the vast majority of inland Australia surviving for long periods without rain.
- Mt Remarkable rises from the surrounding wheat paddocks with Melrose at its foot and is one of the prettiest towns *Postcards* has seen.
- A trip to the Flinders is not complete without experiencing the spirit of the land through the people who have been connected with this part of South Australia for tens of thousands of years.
- You don't necessarily need to have a four-wheel drive to experience and appreciate the Outback – you can catch a ride with the Outback Mail Run.
- The gothic-style Saint Gabriel's Church at Cradock rises incongruously from a paddock, but it's the perfect place for a murder mystery dinner or a wedding with a difference.

Tips From the Crew

- Jeff recommends taking your binoculars when you travel. He says the sky over the northern Flinders is so dark and clear that you can often see far-off planets and stars.

- Ron says the Arkaroola Wilderness Sanctuary abounds with wildlife and if you're lucky you'll see many of the 160 species of birds found there.

- Lisa suggests bed and breakfast at the legendary Prairie Hotel at Parachilna. She says it's a desert oasis and the surrounding property has been used as a location in many feature films.

The vast landscape of the Flinders and outback is constantly changing

Photo by Pete Dobré

The *Postcards* team has spent a lot of time in the Flinders and beyond and every time we come back we begin planning our next trip – such is the magical power of the vast Australian Outback.

Want More Information?

SA Visitor and Travel Centre
1300 655 276

Flinders Ranges/Outback Visitor Hotline
1800 633 060

Port Augusta, Flinders/Outback Visitor Centre
(08) 8641 0793

Free Outback Touring Guide
1800 633 060 or
www.theoutback.com.au

Road Conditions Hotline
1300 361 033

National Parks and Wildlife SA
(08) 8648 4244

RAA Touring (maps and guides)
(08) 8202 4600

SA Tourism Commission website
www.southaustralia.com

***Postcards* website**
www.postcards.sa.com.au

I Didn't Know That!

• South Australia produces 85 per cent of the world's opals – most of them are found around Coober Pedy, Andamooka and Mintabie.

• Lake Eyre is sixteen metres below sea level and is the lowest point in Australia. In 1964 Scottish speedster Donald Campbell set a new world land speed record there, recording 403.1 miles per hour in his Bluebird car on the dry salt pan.

• The group of people known as the Afghan cameleers who lived and worked in the Outback from around the 1860s, mostly originated from the Pushtu tribal areas of Afghanistan and Pakistan.

Arid Lands Botanic Garden
with Mike Keelan

With superb views to the Flinders Ranges the garden features plants that cover most of inland Australia

Two-thirds of Australia is arid which means it receives less than 250 millimetres of rain a year, and because only about one-third of us live in the drier regions most of us miss out on the beauty of the arid country.

That can be remedied with a visit to the Australian Arid Lands Botanic Garden just outside Port Augusta. Set on 250 hectares between the Flinders Ranges and Spencer Gulf, the garden is a wonderful showcase of the plants that cover most of our continent.

The garden dates back to 1981 when John Zwar, Port Augusta's first parks and gardens superintendent, suggested such a garden was overdue. The Port Augusta Council liked the idea and with help from the Adelaide Botanic Gardens, governments, Western Mining and a local Friends group, the gates were opened in 1996.

Now there are more than 500 different plant species and hundreds of types of birds and reptiles. There's a twelve-kilometre walking trail and an award-winning interpretative centre built of rammed earth and 'galvo' that incorporates lots of energy and water-saving features.

The award-winning interpretive centre is built of rammed earth and galvo

Sites of Aboriginal significance within the botanic garden are protected, including an ancient trading post where the region's five Aboriginal groups once gathered. From one of two lookouts you can see the red sandhill where, in 1802, Matthew Flinders stood and looked at the ranges that would eventually bear his name. There's also a vegetative tribute to another early explorer in the form of the state emblem, the Sturt Desert Pea.

I'm always fascinated by the garden's eremophilas – the largest collection in Australia. The word 'eremophila' means 'desert loving' – these plants need very little water and some can even survive for two years without rain.

For me the garden is a wonderful place to study how plants have evolved to cope with salty soils and minimal rainfall. Some have foliage that reduces water loss, some are quite waxy, some have shallow roots and others are deep rooted. They are all vital and to lose some would be to lose an entire ecosystem.

The Australian Arid Lands Botanic Garden is open seven days a week. It's free and is well signposted on the Stuart Highway heading north to Pimba from Port Augusta.

Stuart Highway, Port Augusta
South Australia 5700
Tel (08) 8641 1049
Open daily 7.30 am to sunset
Visitor Centre open Monday to Friday
9 am to 5 pm,
Saturday and Sunday 10 am to 4 pm
Guided walks available
website www.australian-aridlands-
botanic-garden.org

The Australian
Arid Lands
Botanic Garden

Melrose and Mt Remarkable
with Keith Conlon

Melrose was once the Emporium of the North

'It is one of the prettiest locations I have seen,' wrote the explorer Edward John Eyre as he named Mt Remarkable in 1840. Standing on a rise just out of the town of Melrose at the foot of the mountain, we couldn't argue with his judgement.

An easy three-hour drive north of Adelaide, Melrose is the oldest town in the Flinders Ranges. Founded on the strength of a copper discovery, it began with a slab hut in 1848. By the 1850s the town was well under way, becoming the Emporium of the North for stockmen and settlers. It once had three hotels and today the North Star at the bend in the main street proudly displays its claim to hold the oldest liquor licence in the Flinders Ranges.

Melrose used to be the headquarters for the Far North Division of the South Australian police, the largest precinct in Australia at the time. The old police station and courthouse are now the National Trust Museum which is open every afternoon.

In its hey-day, the village boasted three blacksmith shops. In one of them Bluey Blundstone shod the police troopers' horses for half a century and, looking at his corrugated iron and pug-and-pine building, you'd think he'd only just left. It has been beautifully restored and now operates as a coffee shop and bed and breakfast accommodation.

Melrose has managed to retain much of its charm

Photo by Peter Venhoek

Melrose is dominated by Mt Remarkable which rises 963 metres above the surrounding wheat paddocks. The Heysen Trail meanders through this part of the southern Flinders but for those daunted by the five to six hour return trip to the peak there's a less arduous nature trail that runs along the edge of the National Park.

If you do walk to the top the views from Mt Remarkable make the effort worthwhile. To the east, the Willochra Plain is an appealing patchwork of paddocks with puffs of dust pinpointing farmers sowing crops. A short walk down the fire track to the south reveals the Port Pirie Chimneys on Spencer Gulf. Forty kilometres away across the water you can see the white gas tanks at Point Lowly standing out clearly over a saddle of ranges in Mt Remarkable National Park.

Then it's an easy wander back to Melrose which, as its residents proudly boast, is one of the most charming towns in the Flinders. It is also much closer than the vast northern ranges. Call into the Melrose Tourist Park and Information Centre at the caravan park on Joe's Road for brochures on the National Park, its history and the walking trails around Melrose.

Joe's Road, Melrose
South Australia 5843
Tel (08) 8666 2060

Melrose
Tourist Park
and Information
Centre

Aboriginal Rock Art
with Lisa McAskill

As Europeans gradually come to appreciate the magnificent Flinders Ranges we find plenty of reminders of the original inhabitants who have lived here for over 15,000 years.

The Adnyamathanha (Ud-nya-mut-na) people – or 'hills' people have developed a rich culture during the eons that they have roamed over this rugged landscape. Their rock paintings tell the spiritual and creation stories known as the Dreaming and there are a number of tours that take in these sites. We joined local Adnyamathanha guide Sharpy Coulthard on a visit to Arkaroo Rock near Wilpena.

Arkaroo Rock was a special meeting place and was used for initiation ceremonies. It is a gallery of red ochre and charcoal paintings of reptiles, human figures, leaves and kangaroo tracks. Sharpy says other markings shaped like semi-circles may represent the outline of men around a campfire.

There's also an explanation about the formation of Ikara – or Wilpena Pound. Two giant snakes, or akurra, coiled around Ikara during an initiation ceremony creating a whirlwind. They devoured all the people taking part in the ceremony and the snakes' bodies are now the walls of the Pound.

A short distance away is Sacred Canyon where more than one hundred rock engravings or petroglyphs – abstract designs and animal tracks – have been chiselled into the rock.

For local guide Pauline Coulthard, all of the Flinders is a vast story-book of the Dreamtime. Each landmark is part of an ancient tale – like the twin peaks adjacent to the Yourambulla Caves south of Hawker. Pauline says the peaks represent two men who came in search of food. They encountered a wicked old woman who had killed many of their relatives and dumped their bodies in a nearby waterhole. Fearful they would be next, the two Dreamtime companions struck first – killing the old woman. Now the men stand as lone sentinels at a spot pivotal to the Adnyamathanha system of kinship.

A little further up the valley is another series of rock paintings portraying waterholes, campsites and the footprints of the plentiful wildlife found throughout the Flinders Ranges. For Pauline and her people they have special significance:

Markings like these were maps. The people who came through here saw the pictures of the tracks and animals and they knew there was a food source and water nearby.

The Adnyamathanha, or 'hills' people, certainly live up to their name with many of their paintings engraved on spectacular rocky outcrops overlooking the country that has sustained them for thousands of years.

Pauline and Sharpy say the engravings and paintings on display to tourists are probably just a fraction of the sacred Aboriginal stories recorded on rock walls throughout the ranges. Every so often new examples are discovered but many remain secret to ensure their preservation.

An escorted tour is a great way to gain an appreciation of the intimate relationship between the Adnyamathanha people and their ancient land. To arrange a one to six-day tour through the Flinders and Gammon Ranges with local Aboriginal guides contact Pauline Coulthard at Fray Cultural Tours.

To visit the Yourambulla Caves turn off the Hawker to Quorn Road about seven kilometres south of Hawker.

PO Box 66, Hawker
South Australia 5434
Tel (08) 8648 4303

Fray
Cultural Tours

Outback Mail Run

with Ron Kandelaars

The seemingly endless landscape is part of the attraction on the Outback Mail Run   Photo by Peter Rowe

I t's Monday morning in Coober Pedy and locals Peter Rowe and his son Derek are off to deliver another load of mail. But their run is more than a quick whip around the local neighborhood – it's a twelve-hour round trip to William Creek, Oodnadatta and back. The road through Coober Pedy is the last bitumen we'll see for the next six hundred kilometres as we hit the dirt and head east to William Creek.

The Rowes are no strangers to this country. They've lived and worked here for thirty years but they say every trip is a new adventure as the landscape and wildlife is always changing. While we're amazed at how hopelessly barren and inhospitable the country looks, there is a living to be made and it's not long before we come across the divide between two of the most profitable rural industries. The Dog Fence keeps sheep stations on one side and cattle on the other in country vast enough for any dingo to roam free. It's not long before Peter spots one in the shimmering heat:

He's moving slowly through the scrub searching for a feed. Dingoes are wild dogs and they love killing sheep. We probably wouldn't have a sheep industry in the remote pastoral districts without the Dog Fence.

Out here people like to think big and a sign says the fence is over 9600 kilometres long but it's really just over 5500 kilometres. It was built in the 1930s and 40s and snakes its way from the cliffs of the Great Australian Bight all the way to Queensland, stopping just short of Surfers Paradise – an epic achievement when you consider the posts were hand cut and every hole had to be dug with a shovel.

Our next stop is something of a surprise – we come across the Cooreapa Inlet that feeds a nearby salt lake called Lake Cadibarrawirracanna. It may not be the biggest stretch of water out here but its name is apparently the longest place name in Australia. Cadibarrawirracanna is an Aboriginal word meaning 'stars shimmering on the water'.

The lake is on Anna Creek Station, the world's biggest cattle station, covering about 24,000 square kilometres. As Derek points out, that's almost half the size of Tasmania. The station has a population of about twenty but what it lacks in people it makes up for in flies and 16,000 cattle.

After a quick stop to drop off the mail at the homestead, our next delivery is to the classic outback town of William Creek on the Oodnadatta Track. It's surely one of the few places in the world where a light plane can taxi up the main street and park right outside the pub. Part of a British rocket has been erected in the town as a reminder of the role that nearby Woomera has played in the space industry.

Salt lakes are scattered across inland Australia   Photo by Peter Rowe

William Creek has stronger links to an earlier form of transport than rockets – it was a stop on the original Ghan rail line that reached Alice Springs in 1929. The line ran until 1980 when it was replaced by a new standard gauge line from Tarcoola.

As we head north on the Oodnadatta Track we pass a number of station bores that tap into the enormous Great Artesian Basin – the lifeblood of Central Australia. The early steam trains needed a steady supply of water and they found plenty bubbling up from these bores.

Further on at Edward Creek four chimneys are all that remain of the cottages that once housed the workers in a town nick-named Dodge City because of its less than civilised reputation. And our next discovery is the Algebuckina Waterhole. It doesn't look much when dry, but in flood the Neales River turns it into a fierce spreading torrent. It presented a real challenge for the railway engineers and the result was the impressive Algebuckina Bridge. A triumph of steel and rivets and sheer hard work, the bridge travels more than half a kilometre across the flood plain. Derek explains it was actually built in England in the late 1800s and erected here in 1892 to become South Australia's longest single-line railway bridge.

As you travel along the Oodnadatta Track you can't help feeling a sense of history. It follows a well-worn path, having served as an Aboriginal trade route for thousands of

The Dog Fence – 5500 kilometres of manual labour   Photo by Peter Rowe

Algebuckina Bridge   Photo by Peter Rowe

years, and was later the route taken by the explorer John McDouall Stuart as he found a way south to north across Australia. The Ghan was named after 'Afghan' cameleers and at times you see splashes of colour from the native hops, said to have grown from seeds carried in their saddlebags.

Old railway bridges and sidings glide by and soon we're travelling through pink gibber country which brings us to our next mail stop – the famous Pink Road House at Oodnadatta. For us it's time for an Oodna Burger and the 200-kilometre trip back to Cooper Pedy but if you want to learn more about the Ghan the Rowes have a key to the museum in the old railway station nearby.

A trip up the Oodnadatta Track is a fascinating insight into part of our outback pioneering history. If you want to travel in comfort, join the air-conditioned four-wheel-drive mail run tour with the Rowes.

PO Box 324, Coober Pedy
South Australia 5723
Freecall 1800 069 911
Leaves Monday and Thursday

Coober Pedy
to Oodnadatta
One Day
Mail Run Tour

Saint Gabriel's Church at Cradock
with Lisa McAskill

Travelling along the lonely road from Orroroo towards the Flinders Ranges takes you on a strange journey into a little known part of South Australia. Approaching the sleepy town of Cradock with its bustling population of four it's impossible to miss the seemingly abandoned gothic-style church sitting incongruously in a lonely paddock.

Saint Gabriel's is built of hand-hewn sandstone and duly framed by the backdrop of the Flinders Ranges. It was built by the Jesuits in preparation for a big congregation that never arrived. In the late 1870s farmers were madly planting crops around Cradock. A pub followed and, as expectations grew, the Jesuits set to work and Saint Gabriel's was completed in 1883. But the big plans for Cradock weren't realised. The rain didn't come and within a few years the cockies had gone bust so the grand church slowly fell into disrepair. That is until Australian artist Annette Barrette Frankel spotted Saint Gabriel's in 1976 and fell in love with it:

I found out to my horror that it was going to be demolished ... so I spent several years pleading with the Bishop to let me buy it and in the end he agreed. I finally opened it with a great medieval feast.

Since then Annette has been hard at work refurbishing the church and using it for her particular brand of fun – the murder mystery nights which she has made famous at Saint Cecilia's, the former Bishop's Palace and one-time convent in Peterborough. Annette says:

I describe Saint Gabriel's as the 'littlest cathedral in Australia'. It's very gothic and ideal for the medieval murder mystery nights.

Saint Gabriel's was built for a congregation that never arrived   Photo by Annette Barrette Frankel

Annette's guests on these evenings are transported back to medieval times with pewter and silver goblets, vaulted ceilings and six-foot high candelabras. So for an evening of murderous mayhem with a banquet, wine and costumes contact Annette. Overnight accommodation is available at Saint Cecilia's an hour's drive away, or at the nearby Cradock Hotel. Saint Gabriel's is also available for weddings.

Main Street, Cradock
Contact Annette Barrette Frankel
Tel (08) 8651 2654

Saint Gabriel's
Church

Main Street, Cradock
Tel (08) 8648 4212
email cradockhotel@bigpond.com.au

Cradock
Hotel

Yorke Peninsula

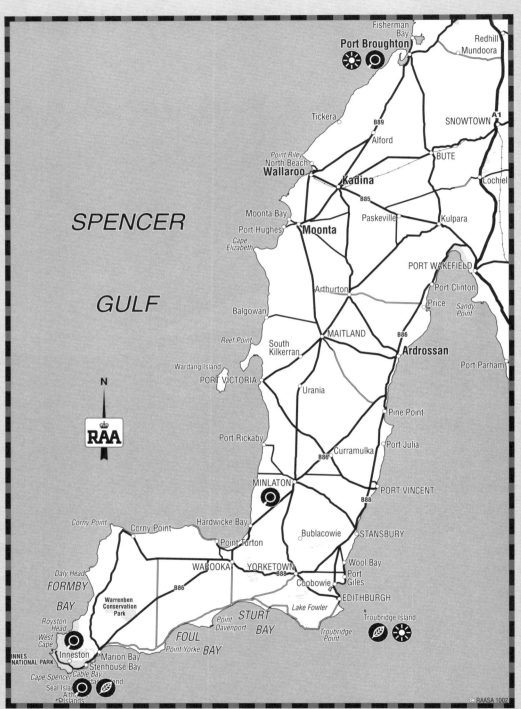

Food/Wine · **Walking/Activity** · **History/Local Interest** · **Nature/Wildlife**

SPENCER

GULF

N

RAA

Fisherman Bay
Redhill
Mundoora
Port Broughton
Tickera
B89
SNOWTOWN
A1
Alford
BUTE
Point Riley
North Beach
Wallaroo
Kadina
Lochiel
B85
Moonta Bay
Paskeville
Kulpara
Port Hughes
Moonta
Cape Elizabeth
PORT WAKEFIELD
Arthurton
Port Clinton
Balgowan
Price
Sandy Point
Reef Point
MAITLAND
B86
South Kilkerran
Ardrossan
Port Parham
Wardang Island
PORT VICTORIA
Urania
Port Rickaby
Pine Point
B86
Curramulka
Port Julia
MINLATON
PORT VINCENT
B88
Corny Point
Corny Point
Hardwicke Bay
Bublacowie
STANSBURY
Point Turton
Daly Head
WAROOKA
YORKETOWN
Wool Bay
FORMBY BAY
B88
Port Giles
Warrenben Conservation Park
B86
Coobowie
EDITHBURGH
Royston Head
Point Davenport
STURT BAY
Lake Fowler
Troubridge Island
West Cape
FOUL BAY
Point Yorke
Troubridge Point
INNES NATIONAL PARK
Inneston
Marion Bay
Stenhouse Bay
Cape Spencer
Cable Bay
Seal Island
Althorpe Islands

© RAASA 1002

Base map and data supplied courtesy of the RAA of SA Inc. and reproduced with permission

Reverse: Old farm buildings between Minlaton and Warooka, Yorke Peninsula

The Yorke Peninsula is one of South Australia's most popular holiday spots – and it's easy to see why. With about 450 kilometres of coastline, and an average width of only 40 kilometres, the peninsula has strong links to the sea. For *Postcards* one of the attractions of Yorke Peninsula is that it is only a couple of hours drive from the city, not to mention the fantastic surfing, fishing and camping spots.

What You'll Find in this Region

• First stop on the *Postcards* tour is Cable Bay where the link between the Yorke Peninsula and the sea is particularly apparent – it's also a wonderful story of early colonial paranoia.

• The ghost town of Inneston used to be home to 'salties', workers who helped harvest the salt from the large salt lakes that punctuate Innes National Park's thick mallee scrub.

• Port Broughton is another Yorke Peninsula town with a history firmly linked to the early farmers and the sea.

• Minlaton might be known as the barley capital of the world but it's also famous for its tribute to one of Australia's early aviators and World War I heroes.

• Thirty-thousand migratory birds call it home every year and it plays an important role in modern day nautical navigation – Troubridge Island has the ideal ingredients for a *Postcards* story.

Black Point, Yorke Peninsula

Tips From the Crew

• Ron says to remember to pack your snorkel and mask to check out the local fish in the sheltered bays.

• Trevor says if you're after a great pizza, try the Marion Bay Tavern where the wood oven pizza is cooked to perfection in an old rainwater tank.

• Keith recommends a wander along Pondalowie Bay in Innes National Park where you'll find a village of rustic fishing shacks and bobbing crayboats.

Pastoralists first ventured to 'Yorkes' in the 1840s but when copper was discovered at Wallaroo and Moonta a decade later settlement really took off. The mining heritage is still a major cultural attraction at the Copper Triangle towns of Wallaroo, Moonta and Kadina.

The Yorke Peninsula has become one of the state's richest grain-producing areas with ports and jetties on both sides. Until the 1940s most cargo and people were transported by ship so it's not surprising there are as many as 85 shipwrecks scattered along the coast.

Over the years the *Postcards* team have regularly visited Yorke Peninsula and we never tire of exploring the incredibly varied coastline. From peaceful holiday towns, sweeping beaches and sheltered bays to the rugged cliffs of Innes National Park there is always something new to see.

Want More Information?

SA Visitor and Travel Centre
1300 366 770

Yorke Peninsula Visitor Centre – Kadina
1800 654 991

Yorke Peninsula Visitor Centre – Minlaton
(08) 8853 2600

Yorke Peninsula website
www.yorkepeninsula.com.au

The Environment Shop
(08) 8204 1910

National Parks and Wildlife SA
(08) 8854 3200

RAA Touring (maps and guides)
(08) 8202 4600

SA Tourism Commission website
www.southaustralia.com.au

***Postcards* website**
www.postcards.sa.com.au

 **I Didn't Know That!**

• The stump-jump plough, a revolutionary invention for farming mallee country, was developed and manufactured by brothers Richard and Clarence Smith, in Ardrossan between 1880 and 1934.

• Innes National Park is home to very rare rocks known as stromatolites, dome-shaped structures made up of layers of blue-green algae. These rocks are hundreds of millions of years old and there are only three places in the world where they are known to exist.

• Early miners at Moonta, Kadina and Wallaroo ate Cornish pasties made with a traditional thick 'handle' of pastry across the top to prevent the workers from getting their lunch dirty.

Cable Bay
with Ron Kandelaars

One of the best vantage points to survey a spectacular part of the Yorke Peninsula coast is from Cable Bay at the bottom of Yorke Peninsula. It's where South Australia's governors landed when they were heading for their summer residence at the old town of Inneston. Cable Bay has sweeping views of the sea and Althorpe Island where, for many years, the lighthouse keepers kept watch on ships passing through Investigator Strait.

'Chinaman's Hat', Cable Bay   Photo by Jeff Clayfield

As we found out on one of our visits, the real story of Cable Bay dates back to when the colony of South Australia was consumed with paranoia. In the mid 1880s Britain was involved in a territorial dispute over Afghanistan. The young colonists of South Australia consequently feared the Russians would invade Australia so they went to extraordinary lengths to protect themselves. National Parks and Wildlife Ranger Richard Thomas explains:

Investigator Strait can be fairly rough and misty at certain times of the year and colonists were afraid that enemy ships would be able to sail by undetected. They decided that the lighthouse keepers on Althorpe Island would be the first to see any invading force so they ordered the island be connected to the mainland by a submarine cable.

It was a big task as Althorpe Island is seven kilometres offshore. Nevertheless, the cable was shipped from London and delivered in two coils. One coil was laid from Cable Bay

Cable Bay   Photo by Jeff Clayfield

to Warooka, 51 kilometres inland, where it was connected to an existing cable link to Adelaide. The other coil, weighing 35 tons, was rolled out into Investigator Strait by two ships.

It's not until you visit Althorpe that you realise what the engineers were up against. Getting here was one thing – hauling the cable up the rugged cliffs to the lighthouse was quite another. The project was completed in 1886 and the lighthouse keepers were then prepared for an invasion that, of course, never happened.

Now it's holiday-makers who invade the bottom end of Yorke Peninsula to enjoy its history and natural attractions. Cable Bay is a comfortable three-hour drive from Adelaide and is on the road into Innes National Park. Althorpe Island is a Conservation Park and visits can be arranged by contacting the local Friends group.

Friends of Althorpe Island
Conservation Park
Tel (08) 8528 5265

Althorpe
Island

Southern Yorke Peninsula
National Parks and Wildlife SA
Stenhouse Bay
South Australia 5577
Tel (08) 8854 3200

Cable Bay,
near Innes
National Park

The Ghost Town of Inneston
with Keith Conlon

Ruins of the old general store, Inneston

few kilometres into Innes National Park at the foot of Yorke Peninsula you'll find Inneston, a ghost town that was once a bustling centre with its own bakehouse, store, butcher, community hall and classroom. The town was supported by a thriving gypsum industry, with workers battling the searing summer heat to extract slabs from the floor of the local salt lake.

A Scottish family in Melbourne knew a lot about the calcified gypsum beneath the salt and how it can be used as plaster for building and decorating when it is cooked. So Bill Innes took a mining lease on the big Marion Lake, only to get into strife in the 1890s depression and be forced to sell up. The gypsum was used to make plasterboard and much of it still adorns many Adelaide homes. Other by-products were also extracted including Bell Co. chalk, made at Inneston and supplied to schools throughout the country. Today the gypsum mine still operates in summer, with twelve truckloads a day taken away to manufacture plasterboard. Originally, however, all the gypsum and plaster from the area was shipped from what was then a major port, Stenhouse Bay, and is now a pretty spot with a great fishing jetty. Inneston was called Cape Spencer until 1927, when the residents petitioned successfully for a name change. When the local lake was mined out, the focus shifted to Stenhouse Bay and during the 1930s Inneston was largely abandoned.

One of the most back-breaking jobs in Inneston was digging for salt. As former 'saltie' Frank Evans reclines on his verandah in Stansbury, he remembers the hard times. 'You couldn't get a job, there were thousands looking for jobs.' With the out-break of World War II, Inneston got a real boost:

Some brainy found out that when they melted the salt it produced certain chemicals they needed for ammunition. So that really helped the salt trade.

Frank remembers both the twelve-hour work days and the advantages of working in a remote frontier town:

We'd go down to the holes in the reefs, take a spud in a jig, drop it down the hole and bang! you got a dirty big crayfish, no trouble at all! But most of the time, it was just hard work.

Near the old stables a sign points the way to a six-kilometre trek along the original railway track, all the way to Stenhouse Bay. You can explore the old mining town by day and stay in one of the nearby cottages by night. Bookings for accommodation can be made through National Parks and Wildlife SA.

Innes National Park
National Parks and Wildlife SA
Stenhouse Bay
South Australia 5577
Tel (08) 8854 3200

Inneston

Port Broughton
with Keith Conlon

P ort Broughton is a pretty Yorke Peninsula retreat midway between Wallaroo and Port Pirie. A picturesque old port in the off-season, it's a growing retirement town that quadruples in population in the summer holidays.

The wide main street leads to the jetty where Captain Henry Dale smashed a bottle of good whisky on a dray on 16 June 1871 and declared it Port Broughton. The explorer Edward John Eyre had passed through the area in 1839 and named the nearby river after the first Anglican Bishop of Australia, William Broughton.

The pylons of the original jetty can still be seen sticking out of the mud. It was replaced in 1876 by the present jetty that reaches out to a deep dredged channel, now plied by prawn and crab boats. In the Victorian era this was where thousands of bags of wheat were loaded – some onto steamships, others onto ketches. The latter acted as a mosquito fleet until the 1930s, buzzing eight kilometres into Spencer Gulf to the anchorage of the majestic European windjammers, that would load up and catch the Roaring Forties back to England.

Each harvest the cargo would arrive via the main street on a railway that stretched sixteen kilometres inland towards the hills around Mundoora. Horsedrawn rail trucks and wheat stacks abound in old photos. You can tell a town was thriving in the late 1800s when it boasted a pub like the Port Broughton Hotel. Overlooking the foreshore and jetty, it was built by Eddy Wall from Wallaroo and his son Bill. The grand 52-room double-storey hotel, with iron lace-work trimmings imported from England, was a sign of the port's prosperity.

About five kilometres north of Port Broughton is Fisherman's Bay, a shack-lover's paradise. The sandy tidal flats are excellent crabbing waters, but fishing in the gulf and sitting on the calm beaches is popular too. Ninety or so shacks are occupied during the year while the other 350 or so bulge at Easter and throughout the summer break. Street names like Garfish, Snook and Whiting reveal local favourites.

Port Broughton's population quadruples during the summer holidays   Photo by Gloria Edwards

Then again, maybe it's a day for a walk on the jetty back at Port Broughton and an afternoon snooze – it's that kind of place!

Bay Street, Port Broughton
South Australia 5522
Tel (08) 8635 2265

Port Broughton
Visitor
Information
Centre in the
Port Broughton
Hotel

The Red Devil
with Lisa McAskill

The beautifully restored *Red Devil* is on permanent display on the outskirts of Minlaton   Photo courtesy Allison's Agencies

The Harry Butler Museum at Minlaton houses a tiny plane known as the *Red Devil*, a 1916 Bristol monoplane made famous during World War I. It's one of only a few left in the world and it helps tell the fascinating story of an airman who became a mailman, Harry Butler. Harry was always destined to soar and, as a kid growing up on a Yorke Peninsula farm, he used to dream of flying.

He was so determined to fly that in 1916 as a twenty-six-year-old, he paid his own way to England to join the Royal Flying Corps and within months was flying sorties over France. A 'natural' pilot he was awarded the Air Force Cross and was soon instructing others. He trained more than 2500 pilots and legend has it he looped the loop over a thousand times.

Butler suffered a head wound during one of the many battles of World War I but his flying days were far from over. When he returned home after the war he brought with him two planes purchased at the military disposal sales in England. One was an Avro Bi-plane and the other, the *Red Devil*.

Soon his barnstorming displays were pulling crowds at shows and fairs around the state. The Minlaton museum has photos of the day he dropped into Adelaide's Unley Oval. But he really made a name for himself on 6 August 1919 when the local Minlaton lad brought the Yorke Peninsula that little bit closer to the outside world by making the first mail run over water anywhere in the Southern Hemisphere. He wore an inflated car tyre just in case he had to ditch in Gulf St Vincent and the authorities had a tug-boat on standby in the Gulf.

But a car tyre couldn't save him on the day in January 1922 when Harry took his bi-plane for a flight over the local wheat fields. His engine failed and he plummeted to the ground and suffered severe injuries.

Harry never fully recovered and died eighteen months later. He was buried with full military honours on 31 July 1924. His beautifully restored *Red Devil* is on permanent display in a giant, glass-fronted building designed to look like a hangar on the outskirts of Minlaton.

Main Street, Minlaton
South Australia, 5575
Open 24 hours.
For more information contact
Harvest Corner Visitor Centre
Tel (08) 8853 2600

· Harry
Butler Memorial

Troubridge Island
with Lisa McAskill

The sleepy Yorke Peninsula holiday town of Edithburgh was just stirring as we headed out into Gulf St Vincent bound for Troubridge Island. The island is about eight kilometres offshore but getting there requires some experience and timing because all is not what it seems.

Our skipper Chris Johnson is careful about where he leaves his boat after we disembark and wade

Troubridge Island, eight kilometres offshore   Photo by Chris Johnson

ashore across a shallow sand bar. The island is part of the Troubridge Shoals and the tides really rip through this part of the Gulf, which means that if you leave your boat in the wrong spot it might not be there when you get back.

These waters have always been treacherous and have claimed many ships over the years. During 1850 seven vessels ran aground in eight months on Troubridge Island alone. The first lighthouse was built in 1856 when a prefabricated cast-iron tower was brought from England and erected.

But it wasn't always a serene life for the keepers and their families as Chris Johnson explains:

In 1902 there was a pretty big earthquake. It must have been fairly widespread because not only did it stop the Glenelg Town Hall clock, it shook the Troubridge lighthouse and started a fire. The light was an oil bath lantern in those days and the earthquake shook the tower so much that it spilled the oil onto the wick and set fire to the lantern room.

Troubridge Island lighthouse and cottages   Photo by Chris Johnson

In 1980 an automated lighthouse was commissioned, the keepers left and the island was declared a Conservation Park. Judy and Chris Johnson took over the lease and have restored the historic nineteenth-century lightkeepers' cottages. It is now the ideal place to live out your own Robinson Crusoe fantasy.

The two cottages can accommodate up to twelve people. You need to take your own supplies but the fee includes boat transfers to and from the island and, as an added bonus, Chris often trawls for snook on the way back to Edithburgh. We left Troubridge with plenty of memories *and* an esky full of fish.

Edithburgh, Yorke Peninsula
South Australia 5583
Contact Judy and Chris Johnson
Tel (08) 8852 6290

Troubridge
Island Hideaway

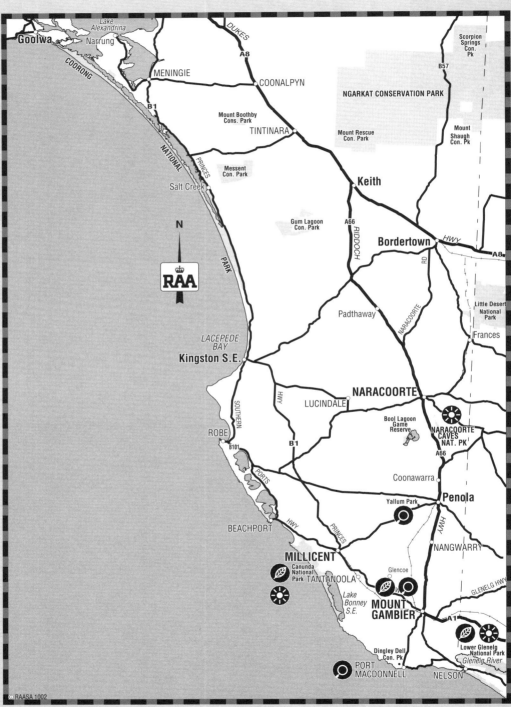

Legend

🍇 Food/Wine ☀ Walking/Activity 🔍 History/Local Interest 🌿 Nature/Wildlife

Goolwa
Lake Alexandrina
Narrung
COORONG
DUKES
A8
Scorpion Springs Con. Pk
B57
MENINGIE
COONALPYN
NGARKAT CONSERVATION PARK
B1
Mount Boothby Cons. Park
NATIONAL
TINTINARA
Mount Rescue Con. Park
Mount Shaugh Con. Pk
PRINCES
Messent Con. Park
Keith
Salt Creek
Gum Lagoon Con. Park
A66
RIDDOCH
Bordertown
HWY
A8
PARK
RAA
Little Desert National Park
Padthaway
NARACOORTE
RD
Frances
LACEPEDE BAY
Kingston S.E.
NARACOORTE
LUCINDALE
Bool Lagoon Game Reserve
NARACOORTE CAVES NAT. PK
SOUTHERN
HWY
ROBE
B101
B1
A66
Coonawarra
PORTS
Penola
Yallum Park
BEACHPORT
HWY
PRINCES
NANGWARRY
MILLICENT
Glencoe
GLENELG HWY
Canunda National Park
TANTANOOLA
Lake Bonney S.E.
MOUNT GAMBIER
A1
Lower Glenelg National Park
Glenelg River
Dingley Dell Con. Pk
PORT MACDONNELL
NELSON

© RAASA 1002

Reverse: Little Dip, Limestone Coast   **Photo by Pete Dobré**

The south-east corner of South Australia is a delightful blend of landscapes – pure ocean water, deep underground caves, craggy coasts and white beaches. Once entirely covered by the waters of the Southern Ocean, for millions of years tonnes of marine sediment built up on the ocean floor and, when the waters gradually receded, the ancient seabed became what we now know as the Limestone Coast. A million years on, that limestone foundation filters water for the enormous underground aquifer, contributes to the region's distinctive soil characteristics including the terra rossa of the Coonawarra wine region, and has led to the creation of the caves of Naracoorte and the sinkholes further south. The unique Blue Lake crater at Mt Gambier is a window into the underground aquifer, and the pine plantations, the grain-growing areas and prime stock country are also dependent on the ancient layers of limestone laid down over millions of years.

In this selection of *Postcards* stories from the Limestone Coast we'll visit a few places that offer a chance to understand the region's connection with its geological past.

What You'll Find in this Region

- We begin at the fishing village of Port MacDonnell for a slice of colonial culture at the former home of poet and legendary horseman Adam Lindsay Gordon.
- Then we venture to the centre of the region at Naracoorte and the World Heritage-listed Naracoorte Caves.
- At the 'capital' of the Limestone Coast, Mt Gambier, we'll explore the majestic Blue Lake and ask 'why is it so blue?'
- A pleasant drive through the pine forests sees us cruising the majestic Glenelg River.
- The Riddoch Highway takes us through the spectacular wine regions of Padthaway and Coonawarra to Penola, where we call in at the grand mansion of the 'Father of the Coonawarra', John Riddoch.
- Later we'll go on an adventure in the Canunda National Park to learn about the region's original inhabitants and hear tales of shipwrecks and survival.

Tips From the Crew

- Lisa suggests a trip to Wilsons at Robe in the main street of the town, where you'll find a stunning range of local arts and crafts.

- Jeff says you should drop in to the family-run Zema Estate in the Coonawarra, for delicious red wine and homemade olive oil.

- If you're looking for opera on the sound system, modern architecture and a bush yarn, Keith suggests you call in on the 'Prof' at Majella Wines in the Coonawarra.

Cruising the majestic Glenelg River

Want More Information?

SA Visitor and Travel Centre
1300 655 276

Limestone Coast Visitor Information
1800 087 087

Limestone Coast website
www.thelimestonecoast.com

National Parks and Wildlife SA
(08) 8735 1111

RAA Touring (maps and guides)
(08) 8202 4600

SA Tourism Commission website
www.southaustralia.com

***Postcards* website**
www.postcards.sa.com.au

I Didn't Know That!

• The seventeen-metre giant lobster that welcomes visitors to Kingston is nicknamed 'Larry'.

• The Coorong National Park is home to the largest breeding colony of pelicans in Australia.

• In 1859, 87 people died in the wreck of the *Admella*, off Carpenter's Rocks.

• In 1857 thousands of Chinese men landed at Robe and walked to the Victorian goldfields to avoid paying a tax for landing in Melbourne.

Adam Lindsay Gordon's Cottage
with Ron Kandelaars

Adam Lindsay Gordon

O nce regarded as Australia's greatest poet, Adam Lindsay Gordon's life story reads like one of his own galloping pieces of verse. Described as a riotous youth, Gordon was shipped off to Adelaide by his parents from their Scottish estate in 1853. Not long after he arrived he signed up as a horse breaker with the mounted police at the Thebarton barracks in Adelaide before being posted to Penola as a trooper. It proved to be the ideal posting for this most unusual policeman.

His passions were poetry and horse riding and the locals often heard him quoting a verse or two as he rode by. After leaving the mounted police in 1865 he stayed in the South East and, by visiting his quaint holiday cottage known as Dingley Dell at Port MacDonnell, it's not hard to see why.

Built in 1862, Adam Lindsay Gordon bought the colonial cottage for 150 pounds. Later it was the first house to be put on South Australia's Heritage Register.

Dingley Dell was the first house to be placed on South Australia's Heritage Register   Photo by Allan Childs

During his time there Gordon wrote poetry, became a state member of parliament and enhanced his reputation as a horseman with feats of daring. It's claimed he jumped his horse over a fence and onto a narrow ledge on the edge of the Blue Lake crater. His poetry is full of swashbuckling themes – midnight rides and tales of brave stockmen.

Allan Childs, the man who lovingly maintains Dingley Dell, believes Adam Lindsay Gordon's verse contributed to an early sense of nationhood in Australia. He says a passage from the 1865 poem 'Ye Wearie Wayfarer' best sums up Adam Lindsay Gordon's character:

Life is mostly froth and bubble,
Two things stand like stone.
Kindness in another's trouble,
Courage in your own.

Old photos displayed at Dingley Dell reveal the extent of his fame well after his death, with the cottage becoming somewhat of a shrine in the 1930s when hundreds gathered for broadcasts of Gordon's poetry.

His fame extended beyond Australia's shores too. At Dingley Dell you can see correspondence from American president Theodore Roosevelt in which he describes himself as an old admirer of Gordon's poetry and states his liking for another poet by the name of Banjo Patterson.

Gordon's fame reached its peak in 1934 when, sixty-four years after his death, a bust of the balladeer was installed in Poet's Corner in Westminster Abbey. He is the only Australian poet to receive such an honour.

But such posthumous celebration belies the tragedies that plagued Gordon's later life. He moved to Ballarat from Port MacDonnell and bought a livery stable but that investment went up in flames in a bad fire. Then his eleven-month-old baby, Annie, died and his wife, Maggie, left him. Gordon moved to Melbourne where, no longer allowed to compete in steeplechase events because of head injuries he'd suffered in falls, he took a job as a sports reporter on a newspaper owned by another great writer of the time, Marcus Clarke.

However faced with financial ruin when his claim to Esslemont Castle in Scotland failed, Gordon later shot himself on Melbourne's Brighton Beach. In years to come his verse would be recited in classrooms around the country.

Many of Gordon's personal belongings are on display in Dingley Dell Cottage, which is part of the Dingley Dell Conservation Park, so after visiting the house allow some time for a stroll through the surrounding bushland.

Dingley Dell Conservation Park
Port MacDonnell
South Australia 5291
Tel (08) 8738 2221
email dinglydell@seol.net.au
Open daily from 9 am to 4 pm
Special tours by arrangement

Dingley Dell Cottage

Adventure Caving at the Naracoorte Caves National Park

with Lisa McAskill

Lisa in the underground labyrinth of Naracoorte Caves

Equipped with overalls, helmet, kneepads and a torch, we followed our guide down into Stick Tomato Cave and, within minutes, were in a very different world. We were told to stick together and the reason for that advice became clear the further we descended into the subterranean maze. Guided adventure caving tours operate from the Naracoorte Caves Interpretive Centre, and for much of the time you proceed on hands and knees, getting a worm's-eye view of a cave system that the experts believe is about a million years old. Over thousands of years the underground water table has gradually dissolved part of the limestone leaving hundreds of caverns and tunnels behind. The caves were discovered in the 1840s when the first European settlers in the district went in search of lost sheep.

As you wriggle your way through the darkness, you get a distinct feeling that you are being watched. The cave network is home to thousands of endangered southern bent wing bats. They even have a maternity cave where they return each year to have their babies in summer.

While the bats choose to be here, other animals have stumbled accidentally into the caves for thousands of years. Now their remains are part of a World Heritage Fossil Site that is providing palaeontologists with a remarkable treasure chest of information about a world long past.

The spectacular tunnels and caverns have been formed by underground water dissolving the limestone

Some of those discoveries can be found scattered around the cave exit when you emerge into the light and find yourself surrounded by large ferns. For a real sense of what the megafauna used to be like, visit the nearby Wonambi Fossil Centre.

Here you come face to face with the remains of *Wonambi naracoortensis*, a snake-like creature unknown to science before its discovery here. Among other finds are the fossils of a giant carnivorous goanna – so big it could have looked you in the eye. As well as evidence of creatures like the massive *Diprotodon*, a giant wombat-like marsupial once common across Australia and weighing a massive two-and-a-half tonnes. Just what wiped all of these animals out no one knows for sure, but the fossils found in caves like the ones at Naracoorte will keep the scientists busy for many years to come.

Adventure Caving Tours at Naracoorte leave from the Wonambi Fossil Centre. Bookings are essential and the cost includes equipment hire. After that, if you want a longer adventure there are extended tours of Fox Cave or Starburst Chamber that have advanced eco-tourism accreditation.

Wonambi Fossil Centre
General Cave Tours
and Adventure Caving
Tel (08) 8762 2340
Open daily 9 am to 5 pm

Naracoorte
Caves National
Park
(10 kilometres
south of
Naracoorte)

Aquifer Tours at Mt Gambier's Blue Lake

with Keith Conlon

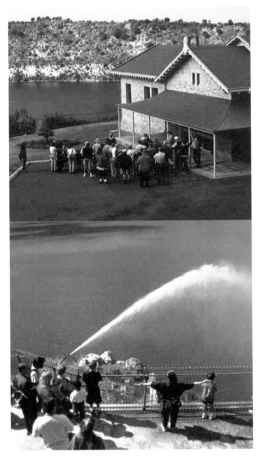

Mt Gambier took its name from the highest point of a nearby extinct volcanic crater but when you visit the capital of the Limestone Coast it's easy to see why it's better known as the Blue Lake City.

After all, the lake inside the crater is the main attraction. The lake's mysterious deep blue water has been filtered underground as it passes slowly through the limestone beneath the city. From any vantage point around the three-and-a-half kilometre circumference of the crater the colour of the water is stunning – as long as you come between November and March, that is.

The best way to see the lake is by joining Garry Turner's award-winning

The colour of the Blue Lake becomes more fascinating the closer you get to the surface
Photos by Garry Turner

hourly Aquifer Tour. It's as easy as turning up at the entry to the Blue Lake on John Watson Drive. While Garry's an enthusiastic guide full of information about the pumping system, folklore, Aboriginal Dreaming stories and the lake's marine life, he admits the star of the show is the lake itself.

The descent to the lake's surface is an attraction too. We travel in a glass lift down a well that was cut through the crater wall to supply the town with water in the 1880s. It took five months to dig and another two months to line with hand-cut stone. Now the elevator drops thirty metres to the viewing level in about a minute.

The colour of the water becomes more fascinating the closer you get to the lake surface. In winter it looks grey while in summer it's electric blue – or is it royal blue? While Garry emphasises his explanation is still theoretical, scientists seem to agree that the lake looks grey in winter because of the presence of small calcite particles which rise to the surface and make the water cloudy. In summer the particles sink and the lake turns famously blue.

In summer months tour groups are amazed that the ancient water just below them is so clear and the views across the lake to the crater walls are just as impressive.

It's a fact-filled tour that only takes an hour, but the one thing all Garry's customers are definitely going to talk about when they get home is the magic of the *Blue* Lake.

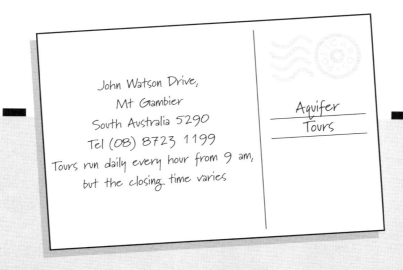

John Watson Drive,
Mt Gambier
South Australia 5290
Tel (08) 8723 1199
Tours run daily every hour from 9 am,
but the closing time varies

Aquifer
Tours

Glenelg River
with Ron Kandelaars

A short stretch of the Glenelg River curves briefly into South Australia   Photo by Harvey McBain

Tucked away near the pine forests of the South East is a short stretch of the Glenelg River that curves briefly into South Australia. From the town of Donovan to the limestone cliffs of the Gorge, the three-and-a-half kilometre South Australian section of the Glenelg includes some of the best scenery along this mighty tidal river.

One way to appreciate the Glenelg is aboard the *Nelson Endeavour* skippered by Harvey McBain. He regularly guides his boat through the lower reaches of the river to the world-famous Princess Margaret Rose Caves. Harvey's running commentary paints a vivid picture of the impressive river:

We're cruising past what are known as the Amphitheatre Caves. They're joined by a chasm about the size of our boat – so they're pretty big. From about the 1870s to the 1920s this is where the Chinese market gardeners used to come to get bat guano fertiliser for their gardens in Mt Gambier.

The Glenelg River stretches 440 kilometres from the Grampians in central Victoria to the river port of Nelson, just the other side of the South Australian border. There are two theories about the river's formation – one is that the gorge was carved out of the limestone by the raging torrent of water that swept through the area when the

Grampians formed a massive mountain range. The other is that the Glenelg River resulted from a seismic crack caused by volcanic activity.

Brackish water extends 50 kilometres upstream but there's also plenty of fresh water. During the cruise Harvey takes the boat alongside one of the largest freshwater springs that feed into the Glenelg. The aquifer increases the level of the river by about half a centimetre a day when the river mouth blocks, usually between Christmas and Easter. These seasonal changes make the river a popular fishing spot. The locals and many a keen angler can attest to that with some great mulloway catches at the right time of the year.

The part of the river that flows through the Lower Glenelg National Park is also a haven for bird life. Visitors can see the small islands where swans take refuge to have their young, safe from feral cats and foxes. The sound of bird song is only occasionally interrupted by the slow chug of an old cray boat. That's because Nelson Endeavour Tours is a family affair with Harvey's father Don also plying the waters of the Glenelg in *Pompeii's Pride*. Don's boat, the *Nelson Endeavour*, and a third boat, the *Nelson Explorer*, offer a great opportunity to explore what is a massive but little-known river at a leisurely pace.

Cruises depart from Nelson, which is just over the border in Victoria and include a visit to the Princess Margaret Rose Caves. They depart daily except Monday and Friday.

Old Bridge Road, Nelson
South Australia 3292
Contact Harvey McBain
Tel (08) 8738 4191
website www.glenelgrivercruises.com.au

Glenelg
River Cruises

Yallum Park

with Lisa McAskill

Yallum Park was built for the man who became known as the 'Father of the Coonawarra'   Photo courtesy Glen Clifford

Yallum Park was built for one of the great pioneers of the Limestone Coast, Scottish immigrant John Riddoch. It's considered one of the best-preserved Victorian-era homes in the country and has a significant link to Australia's wine industry. Later known as the 'Father of the Coonawarra', Riddoch settled in the region in 1861 and made his early fortune selling supplies to the diggers in the Victorian goldfields. He also ran a huge sheep property and by 1880 had built Yallum Park – a homestead at the centre of his emerging pastoral empire.

No expense was spared – it seems Riddoch was determined that his house should turn heads, no matter which room you enter. Of particular interest to some is a stunning collection of 1880s wallpaper inspired by the William Morris Arts and Crafts movement in England.

Glen Clifford knows every nook and cranny of Yallum Park and so he should – he was born here in 1917 and has lived here ever since. For him every room has a story – like the day Prince Albert and Prince George came to visit back in 1881:

Albert and George played on the billiard table. Albert was heir to the throne and he died early and George became George the Fifth.

Back then John Riddoch may have served the royals some local wine as the surrounding region was already well-known for the cultivation of vines and fruit. But it wasn't until 1890 when Riddoch established the Penola Fruit Colony that the scene was set for the Coonawarra becoming a major wine region. Glen still has the original survey map for the two-thousand acres that John Riddoch subdivided into smaller lots and sold to local farmers at reasonable rates specifically to grow vineyards and orchards.

If you enjoy a Coonawarra red, then you should visit the old orchard in the Yallum Park garden. Amid the old figs and quinces are remnants of some of the very first vine plantings in the area. They were struck in the late 1850s even before John Riddoch's arrival. And if you're lucky Glen may even bring out a bottle of claret from the very first Coonawarra vintage. Unfortunately it's empty, its contents were enjoyed long ago – but it is another piece of the past from Yallum Park.

Millicent Road, Penola
South Australia 5277
Tel (08) 8737 2435
Phone for opening hours
Tour costs $5
Group bookings welcome

Yallum Park
(8 kilometres
from Penola)

Canunda National Park

with Ron Kandelaars

As we head south-west from Millicent into the low-lying scrub of Canunda National Park it seems like just another trip to the coast. But as we begin to inch our way across a series of limestone ledges and what seems like a trackless desert heading towards a giant, looming sand dune that locals call the Razorback, we are grateful for tour operator Ross England's local knowledge – not to mention his four-wheel-driving skills:

At certain times of the year the top of the Razorback is very thin. It's like going up and over a razor. At other times it's a very rounded hill, because the sand dune system in the park is always changing. The wind blows and the sand moves and you'll come back at another time of the year and it will be totally different.

That's why it's essential to follow the marker poles – they are the only way in and out of Canunda National Park. The tense four-wheel-drive ride is well worth it once we get to the top of the Razorback and take in the stunning view of the unforgiving coastline.

After the thrill of the Razorback we head to a quiet stretch of perfect coastal sand-hills for a rest and lunch, but we're by no means the first people to have discovered this place's charms. The Boandik people camped here for generations and a nearby shell midden is proof that the region once provided plenty of tucker. Lisa Braes, from the Millicent National Trust Living History Museum, joined us on the tour and explains:

The Boandik people wanted to sit and enjoy their food and obviously around this part of the coastline food was abundant for them. They could find food relatively easily and enjoy the view while they ate it.

Aboriginal middens are scattered throughout Canunda National Park. Ross says the dark flint rock, which is different to the local limestone, confirms that Canunda was part of a trade route extending well inland:

They needed tools to empty their shells – the flint was obviously brought in from other parts of the country but chipped off in this area to make knives, cutting edges and spears.

The south-western side of Canunda National Park is a treacherous piece of coastline that has claimed many ships, including the *Geltwood*. The nearby Millicent National Trust Living History Museum has a collection of remnants from the ship that sank off Canunda Beach in 1876 while on its maiden voyage. All 28 people on board perished. There was quite a stir after locals delayed reporting the sinking. It seems they wanted to offload as much cargo as possible from the *Geltwood* before the authorities stepped in. Rumour has it that some local buildings were later constructed from timber that came from the *Geltwood*'s cargo and, even now, people still bring crockery from the ship into the National Trust Museum.

Canunda National Park   Photo by Ross England

To explore what the early captains were up against along this dangerous part of the South Australian coast, head to Canunda National Park. Ross England's All Luxury Tours operates from Kingston and offer a range of options. The Millicent National Trust Living History Museum displays a variety of local artifacts and it's part of the Millicent Tourist Complex which incorporates a Visitor Information Centre and Art and Craft Gallery.

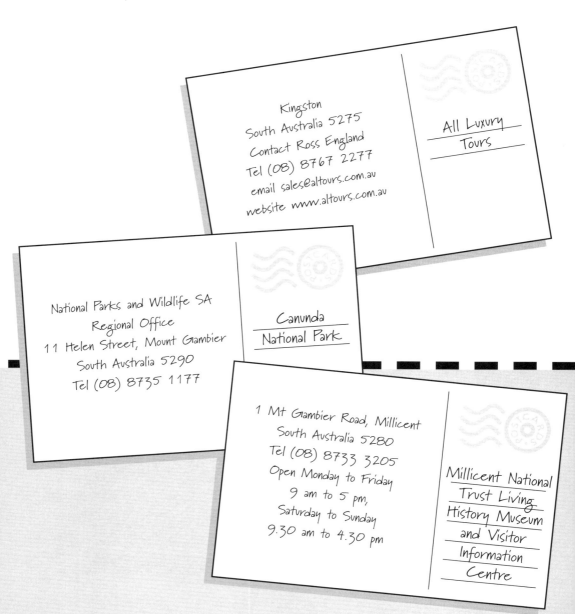

Kingston
South Australia 5275
Contact Ross England
Tel (08) 8767 2277
email sales@altours.com.au
website www.altours.com.au

All Luxury
Tours

National Parks and Wildlife SA
Regional Office
11 Helen Street, Mount Gambier
South Australia 5290
Tel (08) 8735 1177

Canunda
National Park

1 Mt Gambier Road, Millicent
South Australia 5280
Tel (08) 8733 3205
Open Monday to Friday
9 am to 5 pm,
Saturday to Sunday
9.30 am to 4.30 pm

Millicent National
Trust Living
History Museum
and Visitor
Information
Centre

Eyre Peninsula

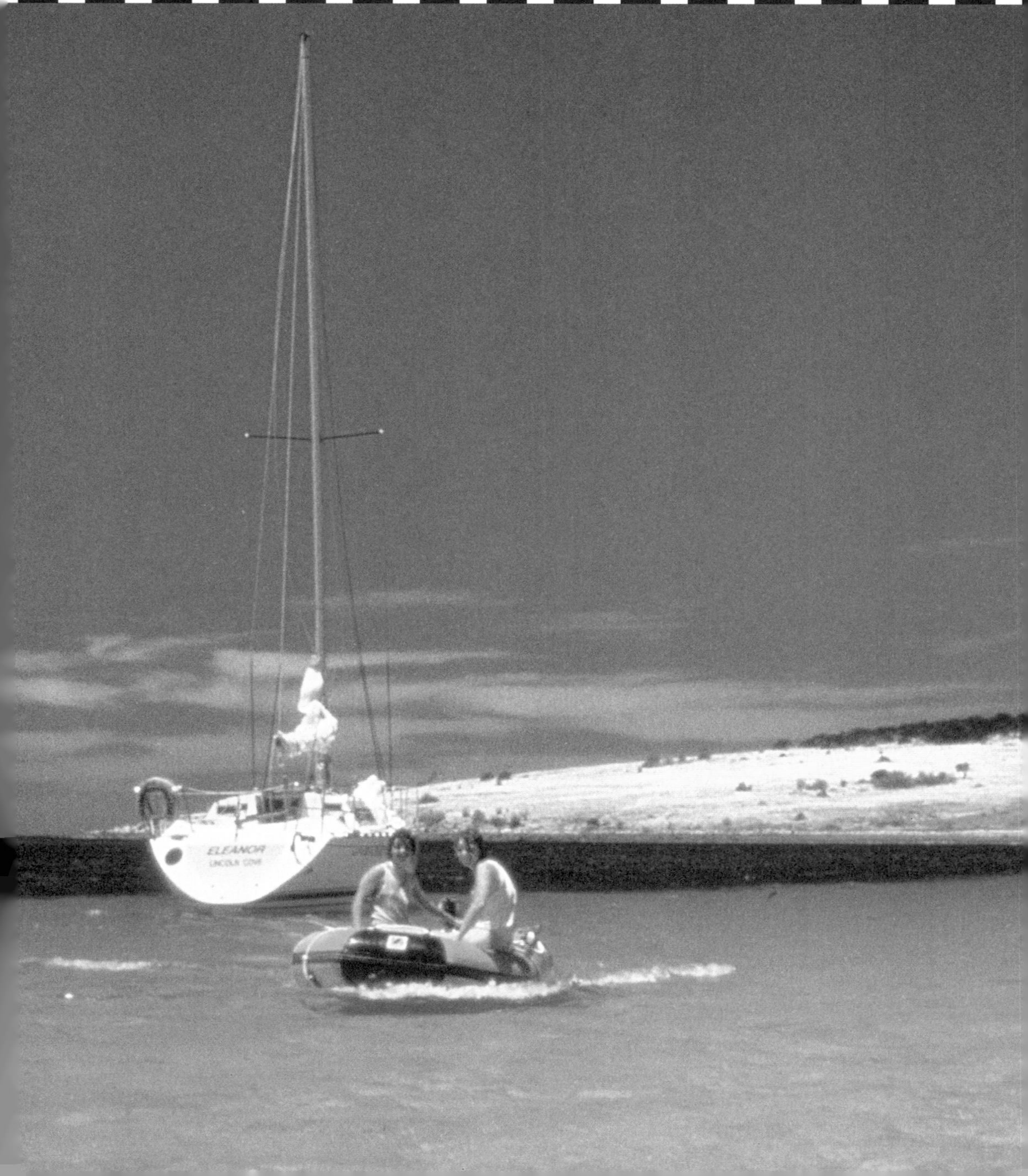

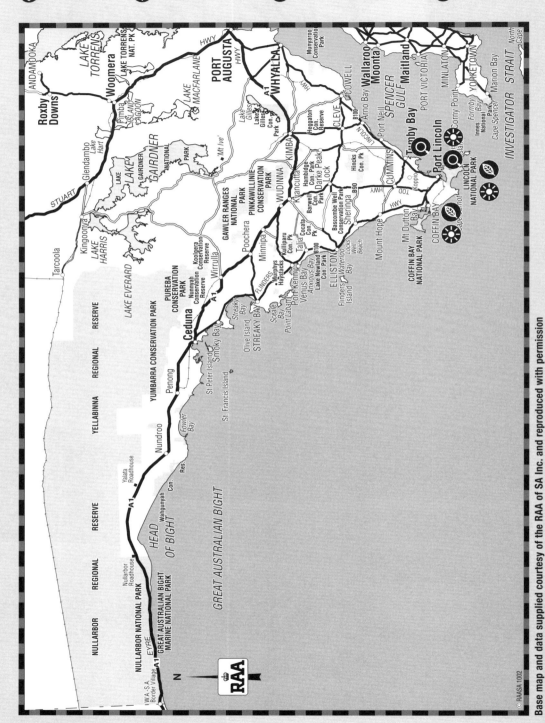

Reverse: Blue-water sailing, Port Lincoln

Base map and data supplied courtesy of the RAA of SA Inc. and reproduced with permission

© RAASA 1002

The Eyre Peninsula is a region with strong links to Australia's early explorers. It's named after the nineteenth-century explorer Edward John Eyre, who made a number of expeditions into Australia's interior.

The Eyre Peninsula stretches from the steel city of Whyalla on Spencer Gulf to the Western Australia border. The Eyre Highway from Whyalla to Ceduna travels inland and skirts around the bottom of the spectacular Gawler Ranges, through incredibly productive wheat-growing country.

What You'll Find in this Region

• Our visit revealed Port Lincoln to be a thriving city perched on one of the world's biggest protected natural harbours.

• The Eyre Peninsula is known for its multi-billion-dollar tuna farming industry, but the Coffin Bay Oyster industry is threatening to steal the limelight.

• Captain Matthew Flinders named many places on South Australia's coast, but Memory Cove in Lincoln National Park reminds us of one tragic event on his voyage.

• Next take the *Postcards* tour of the Flinders Highway, one of Australia's best detours.

• The Axel Stenross story is about a sailor's love for the sea and how it led him to South Australia's West Coast.

Wanna Beach, Lincoln National Park

Tips From the Crew

• Mike says late winter to early spring is the best time for wildflowers on the Eyre Peninsula. He says you'll find Port Lincoln mallee, correas, small orchids, spectacular templetonia, melaleuca, pink boronia and native currant.

• Jeff says the long haul to the Nullarbor Cliffs is well worth it between the months of June and October, when you can watch the awe-inspiring southern right whales at play. Pods of up to sixty adults with thirty calves have been spotted as they migrate to their breeding grounds.

• Lisa says if you're after a thrill, head to Dangerous Reef, where you can arrange to go down in a cage to view great white sharks.

• Ron says as you drive from Coffin Bay towards Elliston, keep an eye out for the Lake Hamilton Eating House. He says you won't get a feed, but you will get a great insight into the region's history – this spot was home to one of the first motels on the Eyre Peninsula.

The coastal road is considered to be one of Australia's best detours because it takes travellers through some of the state's most absorbing and unspoilt coastal scenery. The area also has strong links to English explorer Matthew Flinders who sailed these waters two hundred years ago.

Postcards' wild West Coast ride begins at Coffin Bay and continues east to the Head of the Bight on the edge of the Nullarbor Plain. Through small towns and huge country – farms, cliffs and legends are all big on the Eyre Peninsula, as you'll see from our stories.

Want More Information?

SA Visitor and Travel Centre
1300 655 276

Tourism Eyre Peninsula
(08) 8682 4688

Eyre Peninsula website
www.epta.com.au

Port Lincoln Visitor Information Centre
(08) 8683 3544

Whyalla Visitor Information Centre
(08) 8645 7900

Ceduna Visitor Information Centre
(08) 8625 2780

National Parks and Wildlife SA
(08) 8688 3111

RAA Touring (maps and guides)
(08) 8202 4600

SA Tourism Commission website
www.southaustralia.com

***Postcards* website**
www.postcards.sa.com.au

I Didn't Know That!

• Australia's oldest known rock engravings can be found in the Koonalda Cave on the Nullarbor Plain.

• Mt Wudinna is Australia's second-largest exposed monolith.
• The 1500 million-year-old volcanic peaks of the Gawler Ranges are home to over one-hundred-and-forty species of birds including the magnificent wedge tailed eagle.

• The Sir Joseph Banks Group of Islands is a major breeding ground for the beautiful Cape Barren Goose.

Port Lincoln

with Keith Conlon

The commercial capital of the Eyre Peninsula, Port Lincoln is a magnet for travellers and it's little wonder: the distinctive mallee and seascapes of its nearby national park, the protected waters of Boston Bay, and its position as the most important grain and fishing port on South Australia's West Coast all combine to make it a thriving provincial city.

We began our *Postcards* tour with a magnificent overview of the town and its surrounds from high upon Winter Hill Lookout. From there you get a sense of just how big Boston Bay really is – three-and-half times bigger than Sydney Harbour. The hilltop would probably also have been used by the original inhabitants of this land – the Barngarla and Nauo people, who would have seen the various comings and goings of white people before colonisation.

In February 1802 navigator Matthew Flinders and his crew on the *Investigator* spent ten days in the bay gathering seventy tons of precious water. Flinders' charts of this 'unknown coast' soon brought plenty of whalers and sealers who rested in the sheltered bays.

Today, Port Lincoln's 14,000 or so residents revel in their surrounds, but their number might have been increased hundred-fold if South Australia's first governor, Captain John Hindmarsh, had prevailed. In 1836 he called in here on HMS *Buffalo* and was keen for the harbour to become the infant colony's capital.

Colonel Light rejected the suggestion, claiming there was 'not enough fresh water or good soil'. But within three years, three boatloads of pioneer settlers landed a kilometre or so north of today's jetty. The Aboriginal people called the site 'kallinyalla' or 'beautiful water' and a little shoreline spring still bubbles there today. In 1839 Benjamin Winter did the first survey and the township was laid out. It was originally known as Happy Valley.

The oldest building in the town is the Old Mill, built in 1846. But perhaps there wasn't enough grain being grown locally because it never saw its wind-sails turning above or grinding wheels below. It gets plenty of use now as a lookout with great views

across a harbour dominated by grain silos – gleaming white temples to agriculture. In a good year, the massive silos will store more than a million tonnes of grain bound for the other side of the world.

The Old Mill was built in 1846 and is now used as a lookout
Photo by Keith Conlon

The ultra-modern Lincoln Cove marina used to be all mudflats and mozzies, but in 1986 a safe deep-water harbour was created for the ocean-going fishing boats that help Port Lincoln prosper. The largest tuna-boat fleet in Australia adds colour to the marina for much of the year because their season consists of only a few weeks at sea filling their quota of live tuna for the dozens of floating fish farms behind Boston Island. A number of charter operators take visitors out to the fish farms. After that you can explore some of the best blue-water sailing and island-hopping in Australia.

If a late breakfast and beach stroll is more your kind of holiday, Tasman Terrace, the town's shopping esplanade, beckons. A walk along the old town jetty is compulsory too. Whatever sort of activity appeals, you really should 'take the fresh Eyre' of Port Lincoln.

3 Adelaide Place, Port Lincoln
South Australia 5606
Freecall 1800 629 911
Tel (08) 8683 3544
Open daily 9 am to 5 pm
email info@visitportlincoln.net
website www.visitportlincoln.net

Port Lincoln
Visitor
Information
Centre

Port Lincoln, Eyre Peninsula

The Coffin Bay Oyster Industry
with Ron Kandelaars

Rows of oyster racks, Coffin Bay

There are many ways to experience the attractions of Coffin Bay. In its earliest days Coffin Bay was called Oyster Town and, by 1870, at least thirty cutters were dredging for native oysters in the local waterways, reaping an average 60,000 bushels a year bound for export markets.

Bill Stenson was born and bred in the area and he remembers diving as a kid with his mates in the shallow waters and collecting bags of native mud oysters that they'd take home to eat.

The native oysters have long been fished out but Bill's still here. He and other growers now cultivate Pacific Oysters in what is some of the cleanest waters in Australia. The *Postcards* crew took a cruise with Bill out to the deeper tidal water and, as we motored past hectares of oyster beds, the boom in the industry quickly became apparent.

We eventually arrived at Bill's 'business address' and tied up alongside his oyster racks. For Bill, it's just another day at the office but the only suit you're likely to see him in is a wetsuit. A flat-bottomed boat bobbing on crystal-clear water surrounded by the magnificent scenery of Coffin Bay National Park on one side and rolling farm land on the other seems like the perfect place to earn a living.

When Bill, a former commercial fisherman, bought his oyster lease he transferred part of his stock from the shallow, warm water near the town of Coffin Bay to the deeper water further out, and the oysters appear to relish the move. He reckons they do particularly well here because there is almost constant tidal movement – four or five times greater than in the inner bays. Happy to give us a quick lesson in oyster economics Bill reached into a basket tethered to the underwater racks and pulled out a 'seed' or 'spat' – a baby oyster about one-centimetre in diameter. It's the average size of the growing stock, the majority of which come from Tasmanian breeders. Under the ideal conditions here they will be ready for harvest within two years. Each fully-grown oyster represents a grand total of thirty-two cents, which adds up to a pretty good living.

As you cruise the waters of Coffin Bay, reminders of the past are everywhere. There's the Old Mount Dutton Bay Woolshed, which once handled the clip from twenty thousand sheep and had ketches coming in regularly to take on the bales. The fishing and wildlife is a dream and it's always possible to find a sheltered beach free of footprints.

Or you could take a stroll along a walking trail known as the Oyster Walk, which meanders around one of the prettiest estuaries in Australia. The eight-kilometre path passes many picturesque inner bays and an assortment of seaside shacks and moorings.

Exploring the Coffin Bay area from land is one thing, but a trip on the water lets you uncover the real secrets of this magnificent region. Its beauty and the relaxed lifestyle explains why more people are making their way here and why the quaint shacks now compete with grander holiday houses. You can experience the views from the water with Coffin Bay Fishing Charters and they also offer a fascinating tour of the oyster leases where you can buy oysters straight off the racks – you can't possibly get any fresher than that!

Contact Glenn Boucher
Tel (08) 8685 4355
Mob 0428 912 504
email coffinbayfishing@hotmail.com

Coffin Bay
Fishing Charters

Esplanade, Coffin Bay
South Australia 5607
Tel (08) 8685 4057
Open 7.30 am to 8 pm daily

Coffin Bay
Visitor
Information
Centre

Lincoln National Park
with Ron Kandelaars

Memory Cove, Lincoln National Park

The Lincoln National Park at the southern tip of Eyre Peninsula is a wonderful mix of coastal mallee, stunning ocean coastline, wilderness and wildlife and, as we made our way through the giant sand dunes at the eastern edge of Sleaford Bay, it became clear why parts of the park are strictly four-wheel-drive country only.

This is a dangerous stretch of coast with plenty of soft sand and sharp limestone outcrops ready to halt the ill-prepared. That's why our guide, Steve Pocock, says it's important for people venturing onto the four-wheel-drive tracks to have their wits about them. As a local tour operator, he spends a lot of time retrieving people who get into trouble in the rough terrain:

People need to take time to learn how to handle their vehicles before they venture into country like this.

We are lucky to have Steve behind the wheel as he explains how the constant pounding of the waves is slowly adding to the massive sandhills confronting us – the same sandhills that confronted explorer Matthew Flinders two hundred years ago. In 1802, Flinders sailed around the tip of Eyre Peninsula and recorded the dunes in his journal. He named the spectacular coast after a little piece of his homeland –

Lincolnshire, England. At the time he was optimistic about discovering a strait all the way to the Gulf of Carpentaria but, as Steve explains, his first concern was water:

Flinders just had to find fresh water. He was in a desperate state – his supplies had nearly run out and what he had on his ship the Investigator was going foul.

Flinders surveyed the tough environment from the sea and, finding no obvious sign of fresh water, pressed on a little further east and around the point to what we now know as Memory Cove. Today the eerie stillness of this sheltered bay seems to hint of its tragic past.

The *Investigator* anchored here and eight men, including Flinders' long-time companion, the ship's master John Thistle, and midshipman William Taylor set off in the ship's cutter. At dusk on 21 February 1802 they were sighted returning to the ship – but shortly after they disappeared. A search throughout the night and the following three days proved fruitless – they were never seen again.

For Steve Pocock, this story is confirmation of the dangers faced by the first European visitors to our shores:

They were on a thirty-foot longboat and they didn't make it – the first Europeans to record their visit to this area didn't get home. It says a lot about this area – it's pretty dangerous.

Flinders named Memory Cove after the eight sailors who died. He also had a copper plate engraved. The original is now in Adelaide, but the replica tells the story in Latin and includes a warning, *nautici cavete* – sailors beware. Flinders also named eight islands that skirt the edge of Lincoln National Park after his vanished men. From a vantage point above Memory Cove you can see Thistle and Taylor islands and others named for the 'active and useful young men' as Flinders described them – Williams, Lewis, Hopkins, Grindal, Little and Smith.

Flinders' search for water continued and was eventually rewarded further north in what is now Boston Bay near Port Lincoln. But the tragedy left its mark on Matthew Flinders and on the map of South Australia, when he named the southern-most point of the park Cape Catastrophe.

Soon after Flinders' charts became public, whalers and sealers were sailing the waters and also leaving reminders of their presence.

Surf fishing at Locks Well

One of these is the 'four foot datum marker' – a reference point for measuring the tide. A rock is engraved with a back-to-front number four and Steve reckons it's probably the work of a semi-literate early seafarer.

Behind the engraving Steve shows us a vital part of any remote community – a 'post box' that served the locals long before Australia Post:

It's known as the Whaleman's Post Rock. There's a hole in a big rock and it was where the whalers and sealers left messages for each other.

Until the late 1950s, parts of the Lincoln National Park were grazed and cropped. Now these clearings provide the ideal setting to watch the abundant wildlife like emus and western grey kangaroos. There are also plenty of walks, great fishing and spectacular tracks suitable for both two and four-wheel-drive vehicles. Lincoln National Park has camping and cottage accommodation on Cape Donington but permits are required so contact National Parks and Wildlife or the Port Lincoln Visitor Information Centre for details.

Steve Pocock's Great Australian Bight Safaris offer a range of trips to this part of South Australia.

30 Baillie Drive, Port Lincoln
South Australia 5606
Contact Steve and Rosemary Pocock
Freecall 1800 352 750
Tel (08) 8682 2750
email info@greatsafaris.com.au
website www.greatsafaris.com.au

Great Australian
Bight Safaris

3 Adelaide Place, Port Lincoln
South Australia 5606
Freecall 1800 629 911
Tel (08) 8683 3544
Open daily 9 am to 5 pm
email info@visitportlincoln.net
website www.visitportlincoln.net
Memory Cove Wilderness Area
requires key and permit available from
the Visitor Information Centre

Port Lincoln
Visitor
Information
Centre

Touring the Flinders Highway
with Lisa McAskill

E ven though it's 200 years since Matthew Flinders charted the west coast of Eyre Peninsula, it still has the rugged quality that unnerved the crew of the *Investigator* and inspired placenames like Point Avoid and Reef Point.

A roadside stop on the spectacular Flinders Highway

Now we can survey the same coast from the comfort of the Flinders Highway. It's considered one of the most beautiful road trips in South Australia and we begin in Port Lincoln at sparkling Boston Bay. We'll drive across the peninsula, past Coffin Bay, and continue north-west along the coast to Ceduna about 400 kilometres away.

Our first stop is Locks Well where we get our first peek at the rugged coastline that lies ahead. The lookout gives a stunning view of the spectacular cliffs. We descend the 278 steps of the 120-metre wooden staircase to the surf beach below. It's famous for its salmon fishing and even on the wildest days you are likely to find a keen angler or two.

As we head further north the jagged shoreline is a constant reminder of how many ships found their final resting place along the West Coast. Few stretches of water are more treacherous than beautiful Waterloo Bay at Elliston. Encircled by Point Wellington and Point Wellesly, it looks peaceful enough on a calm day but, as local Craig Haslam explains, the entrance to Waterloo Bay is a treacherous piece of water:

The ships had to negotiate a big reef between the two points. The first ketch to succeed was the Spindrift in 1881. Ketches would come in to pick up cereal and other produce but a number of them didn't make it. They hit the reef and sank.

A mural in Elliston tells the story of a settlement greatly influenced by pioneering governess, writer and teacher, Miss Ellen Liston. The town was named in her honour – 'Ellie's Town' was officially gazetted in 1878.

Today, Elliston is famous for great fishing and surf and we see why at nearby 'Blackfellows' surf break which has some of the best waves in Australia. A cliff-top drive takes us to what Flinders called Anxious Bay because, as Craig points out, there's plenty to bump into beyond the breakers. But the bay has many moods:

Most days you can see Waldegrave Island about four kilometres offshore and on a clear day you can pick out Flinders Island, which is 35 kilometres off the coast.

Forty kilometres further north and we come across a series of strange coastal land formations. A collapsed limestone crater, it's possible to climb down to the floor of the

The rugged shoreline is a reminder of the many ships that came to grief along the West Coast   Photo by Trevor Griscti

Tub at Talia Caves. There's also a tunnel under the cliffs that leads out to the surging sea. Nearby is another large cavern in the cliff-face known as the Woolshed. It's the result of erosion caused by the relentless pounding of the ocean.

All of this is a short drive out of Port Kenny which overlooks beautiful Venus Bay. Just north of Port Kenny we took a slight detour off the Flinders Highway west to Point Labatt. Here, at the foot of the cliffs of the Conservation Park, is the mainland's only known permanent breeding colony of Australian sealions. You can watch them laze about from the purpose-built viewing platform.

Back on the Flinders Highway and heading north again with constant sea views on one side and classic rural vistas on the other, we soon come across yet more strange landforms known as Murphy's Haystacks. Constant wind and rain have sculpted massive granite inselbergs, thought to be up to 1500 million years old, into fascinating shapes and forms. Some really do resemble old-fashioned haystacks.

Next stop is Streaky Bay – a coastal town famous for its fishing. It was named by

Murphy's Haystacks, formed by constant wind and erosion

Matthew Flinders after the ribbons of colour he observed in the water. He thought they may have been caused by a river flowing into the sea but, in fact, the streaks are caused by oils leaching from the seaweed.

Our journey ends at the so-called 'capital' of the Far West Coast, Ceduna. It's a remote town overlooking Denial Bay with a population of more than 3500. Ceduna comes from the local Aboriginal word 'chedoona', which means 'resting place'. It's the ideal place to do just that before setting out across the vast expanse of the Nullarbor towards Perth. But Ceduna is the end of the road on our adventure along the Flinders Highway from Port Lincoln to Ceduna. The drive covers about 450 kilometres (including the detour) and can be done in a day. But to really do it justice we reckon it's best to have an overnight stop along the way – then you can really soak up the magic of the wild West Coast.

3 Adelaide Place, Port Lincoln
South Australia 5606
Freecall 1800 629 911
Tel (08) 8683 3544
Open daily 9 am to 5 pm
email info@visitportlincoln.net
website www.visitportlincoln.net

Port Lincoln
Visitor
Information
Centre

Axel Stenross Maritime Museum
with Keith Conlon

You can't take the 'port' out of Port Lincoln, and it was the old windjammer wharf that brought one of the town's most loved identities here to stay. Finnish-born sailor Axel Stenross liked what he saw on a visit to Port Lincoln, and came back to establish a boatyard on the shores of Boston Bay. Today we can visit the place named in his memory, the Axel Stenross Maritime Museum.

For more than fifty years, Axel Stenross built and repaired boats here. Long-time enthusiast Tom Bascombe took the *Postcards* team into Axel's jam-packed shed to soak up the flavour and tell us a bit about the man:

Axel was born in Finland and went to sea when he was twelve. He was a trained boat-builder and sailed on the windjammers for years. He came to Port Lincoln a couple of times and the second time, in 1927, he stayed. His first yard was closer to town and then, in 1940, he bought this one and shifted his little galvanised iron shack here on a barge. You can see the picture of it on the wall.

Axel and his Finnish seafaring mate Frank Laakso made 250 dinghies and more than forty boats, including his beloved *Rio Rita* that it is now in dry dock at the museum. The small cabin-cruiser work-boat went to the rescue of many an ailing ship and, with Axel as vice commodore, it always led the sail-past of the sailing club.

Another prized maritime piece sits high and dry above the tide in the museum. The last wooden ketch to operate in South Australian waters, *Hecla*, was built in Port Adelaide in 1903, and by the 1960s she was supplying Thistle Island's sheep station in Spencer Gulf. Her unique, bush-windmill-driven bilge pump failed and she sank at the island jetty twenty years back, only to be floated and acquired for this marine collection.

Inside the display and boat-busy shed, Tom showed us an invaluable legacy:

Axel Stenross built and repaired boats in his shed for over fifty years

This was Axel's own set of boat-building tools. Some of these came from his grandfather in Finland, and so they're around 150 years old.

Axel worked every day until he fell ill at eighty-four, and reluctantly left his house to die in hospital. His friends then rallied to create a museum that salutes not only Axel Stenross, but also the great sailing ship era that saw the windjammers calling into the port along the bay until half-way through the twentieth century.

97 Lincoln Highway, Port Lincoln
South Australia, 5606
Tel (08) 8682 2963
email axelstenross@centralonline.com.au
Open September to April:
Tuesday, Thursday, Saturday, Sunday
and public holidays 1 pm to 5 pm.
For visits during May to August please
check in advance.
Other openings by appointment.

Axel Stenross
Maritime
Museum

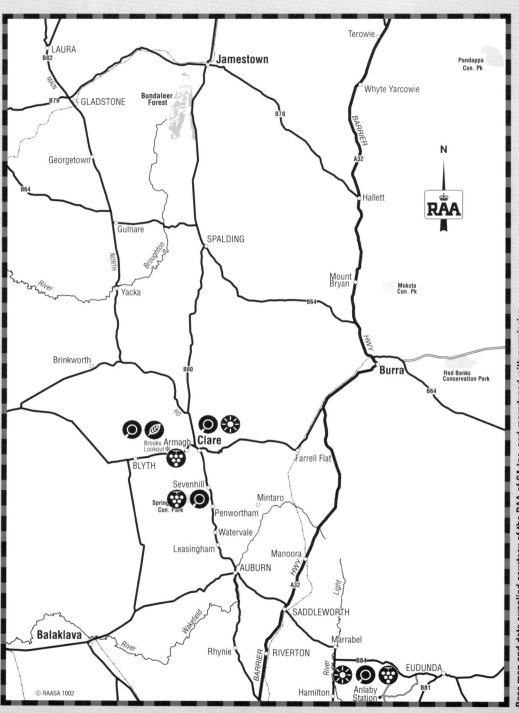

Food/Wine   Walking/Activity   History/Local Interest   Nature/Wildlife

LAURA
B82
Jamestown
Terowie
Pandappa
Con. Pk
MAIN
B79
GLADSTONE
Bundaleer
Forest
Whyte Yarcowie
Georgetown
B78
BARRIER
A32
B64
Hallett
N
RAA
Gulnare
NORTH
Broughton
SPALDING
Mount
Bryan
Mokota
Con. Pk
River
Yacka
B64
HWY
Brinkworth
B80
Burra
Red Banks
Conservation Park
B64
RD
Armagh
Brooks
Lookout
Clare
Farrell Flat
BLYTH
Sevenhill
Mintaro
Spring
Con. Park
Penwortham
Watervale
Leasingham
Manoora
HWY
AUBURN
A32
Balaklava
Wakefield
River
SADDLEWORTH
Marrabel
Rhynie
BARRIER
RIVERTON
B84
EUDUNDA
Light
River
B81
© RAASA 1002
Hamilton
Anlaby
Station

Reverse: Polish Hill River, Clare Valley

The Clare Valley today is home to more than thirty small specialist wineries but the region's history is firmly rooted in more traditional agricultural pursuits. It was once the 'garden of the north' servicing the monster copper mine of Burra. Over the years it has also been an important producer of wheat, barley, fruit, wool, sheep and honey.

The Clare Valley is actually made up of five smaller valleys and includes the regional centre, Clare, and the smaller towns of Auburn, Mintaro, Leasingham, Watervale, Penwortham and Sevenhill.

Sheep, wool and cereal are still grown throughout the region but for *Postcards*, one of the most appealing features of the Mid North is the care the locals take to preserve their heritage – the mining towns of Burra and Kapunda are great examples of this.

We always enjoy a trip to the Clare Valley and Mid North as its sweeping paddocks and rolling hills covered in vines are always beautiful – no matter what the season. No wonder the region attracts nearly a quarter of a million visitors a year.

What You'll Find in this Region

• The beauty of the Clare Valley and surrounding countryside means there's never a shortage of inspiration for those who want to capture it on canvas.

• This region is rich in history and at Anlaby Station we found an excellent example of an era when pastoralists were kings.

• You don't have to go far in the Clare Valley to find a little bit of Ireland, but at Armagh we found a property that also has strong links to Italy.

• Sevenhill Cellars is an important slice of Clare Valley history safely cradled in the arms of the Jesuits.

• The township of Clare was once the bustling commercial hub of the whole region known as the Garden of the North.

Tips From the Crew

• Lisa recommends a visit to Eldredge Winery in the Clare Valley. Ask for their specialty dish 'Lamb and Dam' to eat as you take in the rural view.

• Trevor reckons a stroll around Kapunda's ornate historic buildings will give you an insight into the town's prosperous past. It was once the site of Australia's first viable copper mine, producing 14,000 tonnes of copper metal between 1844 and 1912.

• Keith says if you're after some regional history, check out the National Trust Museum in the old police station on the outskirts of Clare.

Want More Information?

SA Visitor and Travel Centre
1300 655 276

Clare Valley Visitor Information Centre
1800 242 131

Clare Valley website
www.clarevalley.com.au

Clare Valley Visitor Information Centre
1800 242 131

Burra Visitor Information Centre
(08) 8892 2154

Kapunda Visitor Information Centre
(08) 8566 2902

National Parks and Wildlife SA
(08) 8892 3025

RAA Touring (maps and guides)
(08) 8202 4600

SA Tourism Commission website
www.southaustralia.com

***Postcards* website**
www.postcards.sa.com.au

The Riesling Trail, Clare Valley

I Didn't Know That!

• Mid North legend Sir George Hubert Wilkins, born at Mt Bryan East in 1888, commanded the first submarine to travel under the Arctic in 1931.

• Auburn was established in the 1840s as a service town for the bullock wagons travelling from Burra's copper mines to the coast. CJ Dennis, author of *The Sentimental Bloke*, was born there in 1876.

• Explorer Edward John Eyre camped with his party near the River Broughton in 1839 and called the creek that runs into the river 'Chrystal Brook'. A township later grew near their camping spot and retained Eyre's name (although they dropped the 'h').

Medika Gallery
with Ron Kandelaars

Artist Ian Roberts

In the vestry of an old Lutheran Church in the mid-north town of Blyth, artist Ian Roberts brings to life the wonders of the Australian bush. And each day, two resident cockatiels are on hand to inspect his work. It's appropriate that they have the run of the place because the Medika Gallery is all about recording the magic of Australia's abundant birdlife and the plants that sustain it.

A while back, Ian set himself the task of painting all 800 Australian eucalypts and now DNA testing suggests that the total number is closer to 1000, so Ian admits it's become a life-long project:

I've completed more than three hundred so I feel I'm well underway but I probably need another twenty years to actually finish.

It was in the Bundaleer Forest, about an hour's drive north of Blyth, that Ian first came to appreciate the wonders of the Australian bush. His grandfather often took him there to marvel at the diversity of Australia's native fauna and flora. For Ian, a young mid-north farmer and well-known local footballer, it was the start of an obsession that was to lure him from the tractor seat to an artist's studio.

Ian has set himself the task of painting every Australian eucalypt
Photo by Ian Roberts

Brook's Lookout   Photo by Ian Roberts

When Ian's not in his vestry-cum-studio he's nurturing the rarest of native plants in his own nursery. There he strikes hundreds of cuttings from local natives – not just so he can paint them but also so he can return them to their rightful place in the bush.

Ian can point visitors in the direction of nearby Brook's Lookout. For Ian this is a special place where each plant is the inspiration for another watercolour. The stunning 180-degree view over the Blyth Plains, all the way to the Yorke Peninsula has lead Ian to call this spot his spiritual home:

I really believe I 'own' all of the beautiful country I can see from there – but I only own it visually. I think that's one of the differences between the country and the city. In the city you tend to own your own little quarter-acre block and you look over the fence and you know that belongs to somebody else. But for me when I look at the view from Brook's Lookout –I feel it all belongs to me.

Brook's Lookout is six kilometres east of Blyth. There's a picnic ground there and entry is free. You can catch up with Ian Roberts at his Medika Gallery in Moore Street, Blyth. It's open daily.

Moore Street, Blyth
South Australia 5462
Tel (08) 8844 5175
Open Monday to Friday
10 am to 5 pm,
Saturday and Sunday 2 pm to 5 pm
Closed Good Friday and Christmas
Free admission

Medika
Gallery

'Farmyard Boss' by Ian Roberts

Anlaby Station at Kapunda
with Mike Keelan

The manager's quarters at Anlaby Station

About an hour and a half's drive north from Adelaide you enter the rolling hills near Kapunda. This is sheep country, and in the early days of the colony you'd be forgiven for thinking each fleece was golden. There was so much wealth generated by wool production that the early landowners soon established fabulous homesteads like Anlaby Station, originally home to the Dutton family.

Under Henry 'The Squire' Dutton, garden parties at Anlaby were legendary. At one point, fourteen gardeners were employed to tend the grounds, including the 6000 rose bushes. But Anlaby was also a working station with 60,000 sheep scattered up to forty kilometres away. The property is like a small village with many houses and cottages, which were home to the people who worked for the Dutton family – grooms, gardeners, carpenters, maintenance people, shearers and stockmen.

Anlaby was named after a village in Yorkshire, and while for some it was a privileged life, for others it was serious work. The old groom's quarters once housed an army of shearers while other workers bunked downstairs in the old manager's office. From upstairs, the manager kept an eye on the goings-on in the quadrangle below and, at the end of the week, he'd open the safe and distribute the wages to the seventy hard-working staff.

Hans and Gill Albers are gradually returning Anlaby to its former glory. They are only the third family to own Anlaby in its 150-year history. For Gill it's a never-ending quest to tame more and more of the surrounding garden, but I've got to admit there's a certain charm about the parts of the garden that have gone wild. As you walk around the grounds, you can't help but be struck by the grandeur of what was once home to five generations of the Dutton family.

It's worth setting aside a couple of hours to stroll through the gardens and the village, especially the stables filled with Hans' pride and joy, the biggest private carriage collection in Australia.

For many years all of this was the preserve of Adelaide's rich and famous. Now visitors can stay in bed and breakfast accommodation at this hidden treasure, or simply come for the day and take a turn around the property.

Kapunda
South Australia 5373
Contact Hans and Gill Albers
Tel: (08) 8566 2465
Open Saturday and Sunday
10 am to 4 pm
Other times by appointment
Admission charges apply

Anlaby
Station

Armagh Olives
with Lisa McAskill

The Clare region might be famous for its premium wines but if you look hard enough you'll find another fruit in this region that can stir as much passion and interest as the celebrated grape.

Set in the quiet valley of Armagh, about three kilometres west of Clare, is Glendalough Olive Estate. Robyn Hill and Don Hiller's love affair with olives began in 1996 when they travelled through Italy and saw the similarities between regions like Tuscany and Umbria and the valleys in the Clare region. Robyn was confident that their little valley had as much potential for olive oil production as anywhere they'd seen overseas:

We've got almost identical geographical climatic conditions – only better because we don't have pollution. We're also about a hundred metres higher above sea level so the conditions are ideal – especially when it comes to extra virgin olive oil.

Glendalough Olive Estate grows seven varieties of olives

There are now seven varieties of olives in their plantation of 1000 trees. The olive groves are just another chapter in the varied horticultural history of this region. Armagh was first surveyed in 1859 and, as the name suggests, settled by the Irish. Soon it was part of what was considered the fruit bowl of South Australia.

While the hillsides have made way for olive trees, remnants of the old orchards remain. Don's happy to point out the century-old fruit trees at the bottom of the valley that now provide the occasional feed for local birds. In days long gone, the plums, apples and pears were dehydrated and sold, supplying the booming mining populations of nearby Burra and later Broken Hill.

At the back of Glendalough Estate, the old dehydrating room still stands as a reminder of the old Valley of Armagh orchard but the packing sheds have been converted into the cellar and bottling shed.

When selecting extra virgin olive oil, the experts are looking for what they say is fruit, freshness and a peppery aftertaste and, under Don and Robyn's expert guidance, we can all be taught to taste and appreciate the difference.

Whether you're an olive oil afficionado or novice you can savour the delights of the ancient olive and sharpen your palate at Glendalough Olive Estate. Don and Robyn's cellar is in Saint Georges Terrace at Armagh, about three kilometres west of Clare, and is open daily from 10.30 am to 4.30 pm.

Saint Georges Terrace, Armagh
South Australia 5453
Tel (08) 8842 1237
email oliveoil@abe.net.au

Glendalough
Olive Estate
(off the
Blyth Road)

Sevenhill Cellars

with Keith Conlon

Just south of Clare the region's wineries beckon, but there are none that can match the character of Sevenhill. This winery sits comfortably among the Clare Valley's other acclaimed wine producers, but its old stone buildings proclaim its place in Australian history.

The Jesuit community of Sevenhill has been tending vines here for over 150 years and, while the Clare Valley's vineyards are distinct from the Barossa's, the history of the 1851 plantings here also take us back to German-speaking Silesia. Just as the pioneer Lutherans came to South Australia to escape persecution by the King of Prussia, 140 Catholics endured a four-month voyage here in 1848. But why was their Jesuit priest – the founder

The Jesuit community has been tending vines for 150 years

of Sevenhill – an Austrian? The newly ordained Father Aloysius Kranewritter volunteered to tend the immigrant flock and, on arrival, was soon sent to shepherd Catholics from Clare to the huge Burra mine and all the way to the Blinman diggings in the Flinders Ranges.

Over 150 years ago Father Kranewritter and two newly arrived Jesuit brothers found their way here and called their new home 'Sevenhill'. They intended it to be a centre of Catholic culture, like Rome on its seven hills. They even called the trickle of a creek running down the slope the Tiber.

Beginning in a humble hut, they raised funds for a two-storey dressed-stone boarding college for boys by pushing butter across to Burra in a wheelbarrow. They added the money they raised from this venture to a gift from a Munich Mission and gold dust returned from the Victorian diggings and, by the 1850s, the first wing was built. Another wing followed in the 1860s and, in its heyday, fifty-one boys slept in dormitories in the attic with its dormer windows. With priests in training and Jesuits and priests in residence, Sevenhill College was once home to seventy-five men and boys.

Today, an original smokehouse has been converted to a shrine for the Mother Mary and, along a ridge looking across to the college and cellars, a beautiful shrine, built of dry stone, honours the Jesuits' founder St Ignatius.

The Sevenhill cellars and the St Aloysius Church Tower   Photos by Lynton Stevenson

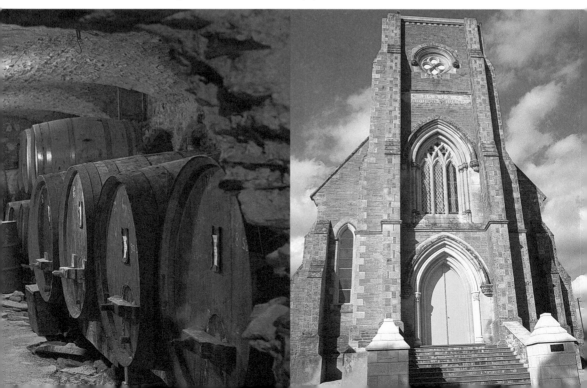

Today, Brother John May is only the seventh Jesuit winemaker at Sevenhill and he's been presiding over the vintage for thirty or so years. An important part of his work is to produce altar-wine for the Catholic Church. Sevenhill provides the sacramental wine – alcoholic and non-alcoholic – for most Catholic churches in Australia and south east Asia. Brother May says the wine is made in a sweet sherry style, according to canon law. They make three varieties, all fortified, so they will travel well and keep in climates like Darwin or Jakarta.

Sevenhill has become an even more attractive tasting experience with its friendly, upstairs cellar door. As the first home of the Jesuit order in Australia, it also offers sanctuary next-door in St Aloysius Church. The simple gothic structure with a front tower took shape over more than a decade, with home-grown graduate (and great supporter of the Blessed Mother Mary McKillop) Father Julian Tennyson Woods laying the foundations of the tower 120 years ago. Brother Waldemann carved the stone detail on one side of the front door and completed the other side after he lost his sight. The towering wooden arches within were hewn from giant redgums, and the massive floor slates were brought from Mintaro.

The church is the first building that visitors see as they approach in search of the cellar door. It reinforces the religious mission of the settlement, which is backed by the dollar value of the wines that travel as far as the United Kingdom and Germany. Fortunately, some of it stays at home for us all to taste at historic Sevenhill.

Sevenhill
South Australia 5453
Tel (08) 8843 4222
Cellar door open Monday to Friday
9 am to 5 pm,
and Saturday and Sunday
10 pm to 5 pm

Sevenhill
Cellar

The Township of Clare
with Keith Conlon

With its vineyards, villages and wineries mingling with bush-capped ridges, the Clare Valley is a picture postcard vista. European settlement of the Ngadjuri people's country began a few kilometres south soon after explorer Edward John Eyre declared in 1839 that this was 'by far the best land' he'd seen except for the Mt Barker district.

John Horrocks, who set up his farm in 1840, was one of the first pioneers and a stone obelisk on the main road at Penwortham tells the story of this 21-year-old adventurer. His farming and exploration of the region soon earned him the title the King of the North, but he was dead and buried in the bush churchyard of St John's church after just six years. During an expedition north he was preparing to shoot a bird when his camel lurched and the gun blast shot off his fingers and part of his face. He was brought back to Penwortham and died three days later.

The best view of Clare is from Billy Goat Hill. From there you get a sense of the town being the grand business hub of the north with its solid stone buildings and well laid-out streets. While it began as the garden of the north, producing fruit and vegetables for the monster mine of Burra to the north-east, it soon developed into the commercial centre for the region.

These days many visitors enjoy the Historic Walk that takes them past many old buildings. The town's first major building was St Michael's church, built in 1849. It was only the third Catholic Church in the colony and went on to house Clare's first school.

The pastoral boom years of the 1870s and 1880s produced handsome buildings all over the state, and Clare has its fair share. Three of the hotels built in this era are still open on the main road. The first licence was granted in 1848, at what is now the classic two-storey Taminga Hotel. The hotelier of the time, a Mr Kenny, recognised the tourism potential and placed an advertisement encouraging newlyweds to leave 'dusty Adelaide to appreciate the sweets of their honeymoon in all its pleasing delights' in Clare. The many bed and breakfast and tourist accommodation operators would agree that there's even more reason to come today.

It all starts with excellent local fruit borne on vines that grow up several small valleys – all 300 metres or higher above sea level. Cold wet winters and hot summers are good for growing premium riesling and since the Australian red and white table wine boom of the 1960s, more than thirty small specialist wineries have sprung up around Clare.

As if rolling vineyards and superb wines aren't enough, the

Clare township from Billy Goat Hill   Photo by Lynton Stevenson

winemakers of the Clare Valley have organised a walking and riding track and named it the Riesling Trail. It follows the route of the old rail line between Clare and Auburn that was destroyed in the 1983 Ash Wednesday bushfires. It's an easy-going 27-kilometre trail that links the villages of the valley. So what better way is there to explore the Clare Valley's many wineries? It's no wonder the Clare Valley lures a quarter of a million visitors or more each year.

Town Hall,
229 Main North Rd, Clare
South Australia 5453
Tel (08) 8842 2131
website www.clarevalley.com.au
email getcloser@clarevalley.com.au

Clare Valley
Visitors
Information
Centre

Barossa Valley

Food/Wine   Walking/Activity   History/Local Interest   Nature/Wildlife

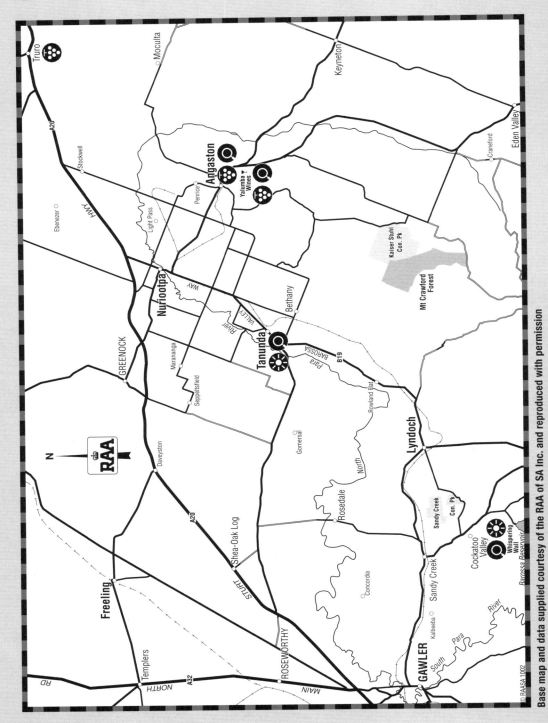

Reverse: Barossa Valley vines   **Photo by Pete Dobré**

The Barossa Valley is probably Australia's best-known winemaking region. The Valley, as the locals call it, stretches about 40 kilometres north from Gawler and is about 25 kilometres across. Several of Australia's major wineries began in the Barossa in the mid 1800s and they still have a strong presence.

But you don't have to be a wine buff to enjoy the Barossa. The vine-covered hills are peppered with beautiful towns like Angaston, Nuriootpa, Tanunda, and Lyndoch. Spend a little time in each and you'll get to see the many faces of the Barossa. Because it was originally settled by immigrants from England and parts of present-day Germany and Poland.

World War I provoked plenty of ill feeling towards the descendants of the many Prussian Lutherans who settled the Barossa Valley. Often referred to as 'Germans', an act of parliament was passed to rename places with German names – Kaiser Stuhl became Mt Kitchener for example.

Now the Barossa Valley's heritage is widely celebrated. Original placenames have returned, menus are truly multicultural and locals proudly boast of their ancestry. We can all experience the Valley's rich heritage through its

What You'll Find in this Region

- Every now and then we come across a little gem and the Craneford Winery and Zilm's Cafe at Truro is one of them. This is our first stop for chocolate cake paired with great wine.
- Lisa tries her hand at kegel – the forerunner to modern-day ten-pin bowling – at the Kegel Club of Tanunda.
- Load up the picnic basket at the South Australian Company Store – appropriately located in old buildings that once housed a fruit packing company.
- The kids will love the Whispering Wall – whether they're aged six or sixty!
- Last stop is Yalumba Winery, a Barossa winery that has been passed down through five generations of the same family.

Tips From the Crew

- If you're into bushwalking, Lisa recommends the scenic trail that begins at Krondorf Cellars and heads along Rifle Range Road. She says you'll be rewarded with classic rural scenery and gorgeous views.

- Trevor suggests a heritage walk around the historic town of Bethany. He says you can pick up walking guides for many local towns at the Barossa Wine and Visitor Centre in Tanunda.
- Keith suggests heading off the main street to find the recently restored Chateau Tanunda which has a cellar door for the Barossa's many tiny boutique wineries.

- Jeff recommends a drive through the Barossa Ranges. He says the view from Mengler Hill is fantastic.

The South Australian Company Store, Angaston

architecture, art, music and food as well, of course, as its famous wines.

**Want
More
Information?**

SA Visitor and Travel Centre
1300 655 276

**Barossa Wine and
Visitor Centre**
66–68 Murray Street, Tanunda
1300 852 982

Barossa Valley website
www.barossa-region.org

Barossa Wine Train
(08) 8212 7888

Gawler Visitor Centre
(08) 8522 6814

National Parks and Wildlife SA
(08) 8280 7048

RAA Touring (maps and guides)
(08) 8202 4600

**SA Tourism Commission
website**
www.southaustralia.com

***Postcards* website**
www.postcards.sa.com.au

**I Didn't
Know
That!**

• Johann Menge and Carl Kornhardt produced Australia's first German-language newspaper in the Barossa Valley in 1847.

• A traditional marriage custom in early German settlements was called 'Polterabend' where friends of the couple banged on pots and pans outside the bride's parents' house on the night before the wedding.

• A mini goldrush occurred in 1868 when around 4000 diggers arrived at Spike Gully after gold was discovered there.
• The Barossa is home to over thirty churches, mostly Lutheran, and many with fine pipe organs.

Craneford Winery and Zilm's Cafe at Truro
with Ron Kandelaars

As the traffic rolls along the Sturt Highway through the northern Barossa Valley town of Truro, drivers bound for the Riverland and further east to Sydney can take a break at a very up-market roadside stop. At Zilm's Gourmet Cafe, Bev and John Zilm prove that long-distance travel and good food and coffee are not mutually exclusive.

The old Truro CFS depot is now an up-market roadside stop   Photo by Steven Baker

John Zilm   Photo by Steven Baker

Bev and John were confident the combination of a cafe and working winery would be a winner. And they were right – the food aromas wafting through the winery create a great atmosphere. John's light and airy wine and Bev's gourmet luncheon platters and antipasto complement each other perfectly.

John used to be the winemaker at Craneford Winery at Springton and he jumped at the opportunity to buy the winery and move it to his home town of Truro. You'll find the cafe/winery in what was once the town's local fire station – the old CFS depot has proved the perfect venue for the talents of this husband and wife team.

Craneford Winery and Zilm's Gourmet Cafe is on the Sturt Highway at Truro and it's worth lingering to enjoy a great lunch with a perfectly matched wine.

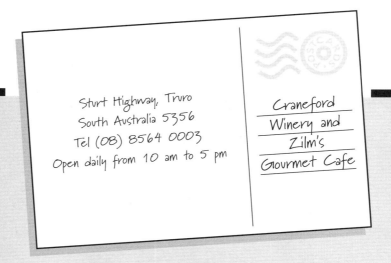

Sturt Highway, Truro
South Australia 5356
Tel (08) 8564 0003
Open daily from 10 am to 5 pm

Craneford
Winery and
Zilm's
Gourmet Cafe

Kegel Club of Tanunda
with Lisa McAskill

With its origins in ancient Germany it's not surprising there's a strong band of Kegellers still carrying on the tradition in Tanunda. A kegel was originally a wooden club that was used as a hammer and sometimes as a weapon, but after church on Sundays it became a target. Churchgoers would stand their kegel in the churchyard and bowl a stone at it, believing they would be freed from sin if they hit it. Up to fifteen pins were originally used in a game, but nine pins eventually became the norm and modern ten-pin bowling evolved from there.

In the early days kegellers used solid wooden balls but I'm pleased to report that these days modern bowling balls with finger holes make playing a lot easier. The day I had a go I needed all the help I could get because the track is over twice the length of a ten-pin bowling alley, and only

The Kegel track is over twice the length of a ten-pin alley

a third of the width. Not only that – the jarrah timbers that form the track are supported by stakes driven into the earthen floor of the Kegel Barn so they distort with even the slightest change in the weather.

Just to add a further degree of difficulty, the track is concave, so it's a bit like bowling down a spoon drain. Good bowlers know how to read the track and adjust their style as the timber moves, sometimes over a single night's play. I was relieved that there is no 'proper' way to bowl. It's whatever technique works best for you, with everyone adopting their own style.

The Tanunda Kegel Club is one of the oldest sporting clubs in Australia, and the building is on the National Trust list. These days there are around twenty-two dedicated Kegel Club members who ensure their game is preserved. Once strictly for men, Kegel Club membership is now open to women. You'll find the Kegel Barn in the Tanunda Recreation Park or you can get more information from the Barossa Wine and Visitor Centre.

Tanunda Recreation Park
Magnolia Rd, Tanunda
South Australia 5352
Competition times: women Wednesday
night from 7.30 pm; men Friday
nights from 7.30 pm

Visitors welcome

Tanunda
Kegel Club

Tanunda
South Australia 5352
Tel (08) 8563 0600
Freecall 1800 812 662

Barossa
Wine and
Visitor Centre

South Australian Company Store at Angaston
with Ron Kandelaars

The South Australian Company Store is set among the vineyards on the outskirts of Angaston and inside there's a showcase of food and South Australian-made products. Owners Kerrie and Paul Mariani drew their inspiration for the Store from 1836 when the South Australian Company was formed to help develop the young colony.

The South Australian Company Store, a showcase of food and local produce

The stylish verandah cafe

George Fife Angas, whom Angaston was named after, was chairman of the original South Australian Company and he was responsible for implementing Edward Gibbon Wakefield's plan of systematic colonisation. From the arrival of the *Buffalo* to the establishment of Adelaide and opening up of the interior, the South Australian Company oversaw a radical plan with lofty ideals which would see an influx of free immigrants from around the world.

Today the Store proudly displays how far we've come. It's an eclectic mix of everything home-grown – from fleece-lined swags to the occasional rocking horse and even terracotta servingware. Once you've filled a hamper from the packed shelves you can picnic in the surrounding vineyards.

27 Valley Road, Angaston
South Australia 5353
Tel (08) 8564 3788
Open daily 10 am to 5 pm

The
South Australian
Company Store

The Whispering Wall at the Barossa Reservoir

with Keith Conlon

The Barossa Reservoir was once the highest dam in Australia, and its bold design made even the Americans take notice. Today it's famous for reasons other than its feats of engineering.

The dam is a hundred years old, but its story begins about thirteen kilometres away in the early town of Gawler. Throughout the nineteenth century, Gawler's water came from a well on the South Para River, but as the quality dropped, fears of an epidemic rose and the search for a reservoir site began.

The solution was novel: in the Mt Lofty Ranges, the Yettie Creek gorge would be dammed with a concave concrete wall twenty-seven metres, or nine storeys, high bending its back against the pressure of thousands of tons of water. The scheme got the nod in 1899 and, by the winter of that year, the construction workers were on the job in the creek bed.

The daringly designed wall is more than ten metres thick at its base, and it tapers up to the width of a narrow pathway at the top. They flew the concrete in, which was mixed on site, by flying fox and added 'plums', as they called them. They were big quartz boulders blown from the sides of the gorge. Higher up the wall, forty tons of old Gawler horse tram tracks were incorporated for added strength.

The dam's design came from Irish-born Alexander Moncrieff, then government engineer. He never took a holiday in forty-two years and he left a considerable legacy including Fort Glanville and Fort Largs, the Port Augusta to Oodnadatta railway line, four lighthouses including the one on Kangaroo Island's Cape du Couedic and a lot more. The Barossa Reservoir however, was his crowning glory.

The day the *Postcards* team visited, we asked Ilsa from Holland to talk very quietly to her friend Frank who was standing 144 metres away on the opposite lookout. To their amazement, they could hear each other's whispers clearly. It's a phenomenon that never fails to amaze and it's caused by a parabola effect. The wall is one sector of a perfect circle, and the sound waves bounce in a series of straight jumps all the way to the other end. Hence its nickname, the Whispering Wall.

With no obvious catchment creeks, where does all the water come from? The answer, amazingly, is a two-kilometre tunnel cut through the range from a weir on the South Para River. It was cut by horsepower – one poor local horse spent nine months working there without once seeing the light of day.

During construction about four hundred workers – many of them with wives and children – lived in a tent and galvo-and-canvas hut town. When the dam was finished in 1903, all that remained was auctioned off and the town was gone.

The dam is worth a visit with the kids – they'll spend the rest of the day trying to figure out the secrets of the Whispering Wall.

Barossa Reservoir via Yettie Road,
Williamstown
South Australia 5351

The Whispering
Wall (follow signs
from main street)

Tanunda
South Australia 5352
Tel (08) 8563 0600
Freecall 1800 812 662

Barossa Wine
and Visitor
Centre

The Whispering Wall is one
section of a perfect circle
Photo by Keith Conlon

Yalumba Wines

with Keith Conlon

Samuel Smith

Samuel Smith planted his first vines at Yalumba near Angaston in 1849 and began a 150-year long tradition of family wine-making. The famous Yalumba clock tower and rough marble two-storey frontage overlooking the Eden Valley Road today disguises an ultra-modern facility inside that produces a million cases of wine per year.

Samuel Smith was a strong Congregationalist from Wareham in Dorset, England, and he probably recognised South Australia as an opportunity. The young province was thriving at this time after the discovery of copper, and he and his wife, Mary, could lease land in the colony free of England's discrimination against religious non-conformists.

The day *Postcards* visited we watched interstate visitors reach for their cameras to snap the great stone and brick clock tower as they made their way to the tasting room underneath. Samuel Smith's son, Sydney, lived just long enough to see it completed in 1908. He recalled his father working in the Angas homestead gardens by day and in his own leased vineyard by night – with a candle stuck on his wheelbarrow. By the third generation of the Smith family, the business was big enough to build the Yalumba landmark building as a gesture of confidence in the twentieth century.

I found an architectural drawing of the clock towers in the family archives stored deep in the old concrete vats of the winery. The 1949 centenary history of the winery and the superbly presented 150th anniversary book, 'Yalumba and its People' are also stored here.

Tearing myself away from the archives, I wandered through the Upper Cask Hall, with its huge oval wooden barrels. This is one of the venues for the concerts and entertainment for which Yalumba is famous – great showbiz names have trodden these boards. And the test cricket rest days in the gardens here are legendary – Richie Benaud recalls how Jeff 'Thomo' Thompson busted his shoulder here trying to smash a tennis ball too hard.

The Yalumba winery now creeps a long way up the rise from its park-like entrance. At the back is a huge old stone shed known as the Octavius cellar. Octaves (small barrels) and hogsheads stacked in rows on the dirt floor hold the premium reds.

Yalumba weathered the difficult times of the Great Depression with the help of American soldiers who took to their Galway Pipe port, along with a shift to red and white wine away from fortifieds, which had been the mainstay of the state's wineries.

Pewsey Vale, Yalumba Winery   Photo by Douglas Coats Photography

Carols by Candlelight at Yalumba   Photo by Milton Wordley and Associates

Now a century and a half on, the company is run by fifth-generation Robert Hill Smith and his brother Samuel. They are well aware that their stories will make up the next edition of the Yalumba history.

The picturesque Yalumba Winery is just out of Angaston on the Eden Valley Road.

Eden Valley Road, Angaston
South Australia 5353
Wine room open Monday to Saturday
and public holidays 10 am to 5 pm,
Sunday 12 pm to 5 pm
Tel (08) 8561 3200

Yalumba
Winery

Kangaroo Island

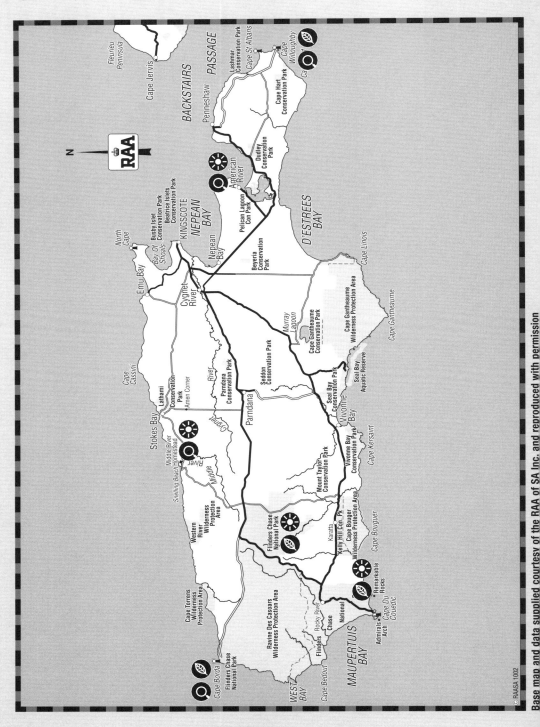

Food/Wine   Walking/Activity   History/Local Interest   Nature/Wildlife

Reverse: Cape Willoughby Lighthouse, Kangaroo Island   Photo by Pete Dobré

Base map and data supplied courtesy of the RAA of SA Inc. and reproduced with permission

Kangaroo Island is another of those places *Postcards* keeps being drawn back to. Every time we step off the ferry at Penneshaw we know we're in for a unique wilderness experience. About a third of the island is national park or conservation park and much of it is as rugged and untamed as it was when the first whalers, sealers and escaped convicts arrived in the early 1800s.

The local people are proud of the place their island home holds in history. They claim the real beginning of the South Australian colony was here. As long as six months before the *Buffalo* arrived at Holdfast Bay, eight ships sailed to Reeves Point near what is now known as Kingscote. Colonel Light concluded that fresh water would be a problem on the island and the original settlement failed. But as if to prove a point, a mulberry tree planted there in 1837 is still flourishing.

While farming and fishing have helped sustain the island since settlement, tourism is stronger than ever and the world's gourmets are now discovering what the unpolluted farmland and clear waters can produce.

Kangaroo Island is only about 155 kilometres long so it is very easy to get around but it pleads for time as its pleasures are best explored and enjoyed over a few days.

What You'll Find in this Region

- It's not in America, and it's not even a river but keen anglers will adore this sheltered inlet.
- Experience the romance of lighthouse keeping with an overnight stay at one of Kangaroo Island's giant sentinels.
- National Parks like Flinders Chase protect many plants and animals no longer found on the mainland.
- Kangaroo Island is littered with places to stay but Middle River Homestead is a true pioneer experience.
- A couple of the island's best-known landmarks are found in one remote corner – the Remarkable Cape.

Tips From the Crew

- Jeff recommends the Rockpool Cafe at Stokes Bay for great summertime eating.

- Ron says if you're looking for reasonably cheap accommodation at a spectacular location, you can't go past the three lighthouse cottages at Cape Willoughby, Cape de Couedic and Cape Borda. He says they're run by the Department of Environment and you'll need to bring your own linen.

- Keith says the long climb up Prospect Hill (or Mt Thisby as many locals still call it) will reward you with a stunning view of both sides of the island.

Kelly Hill Caves   Photo by Pete Dobré

**Want
More
Information?**

SA Visitor and Travel Centre
1300 655 276

**The Gateway Visitor
Information Centre**
(08) 8553 1185

Kangaroo Island website
www.tourkangarooisland.com.au

Sealink website
www.sealink.com.au

National Parks and Wildlife SA
(08) 8553 2381

RAA Touring (maps and guides)
(08) 8202 4600

**SA Tourism Commission
website**
www.southaustralia.com

***Postcards* website**
www.postcards.sa.com.au

 **I Didn't
Know
That!**

• Although Aboriginal tribes have not lived on Kangaroo Island for thousands of years, Aboriginal women were kidnapped from the mainland by sealers and whalers in the early 1800s and brought to the island.

• Captain Bromley established South Australia's first school at Kingscote in 1836.
• Since the first recorded shipwreck in 1847, over fifty ships have gone down off the coast of Kangaroo Island.
• The Kangaroo Island Eucalyptus Company first exported eucalyptus oil to England in 1906.

• Australian sealions and fur seals both have small external ears and can walk on their four flippers, unlike true seals which do not have ears and cannot walk on their flippers.

American River

with Keith Conlon

Pellicans at American River   Photo by Keith Conlon

American River is a beautiful inlet that played an important role in the history of Kangaroo Island. It was named after the American sealers who camped in the area in 1803, a year after Matthew Flinders discovered the island and more than thirty years before South Australia's first official settlement. Led by Captain Isaac Pendleton, the men spent the winter sealing and building a forty tonne schooner called the *Independence*.

The American sealers probably chose their camp because of the protection offered by a low line of hills from the harsh hot summer winds and cold winter sou'westers. After completing the *Independence* they sailed to Sydney town with thousands of sealskins and, after some of the crew apparently blabbed in the pubs, there were five hundred sealers and whalers in the Kangaroo Island waters within a few years.

We began our *Postcards* tour of American River by retracing the steps of Flinders with a long climb to the top of Prospect Hill. Like the navigator, we wanted a high spot to get our bearings although our hike was probably a lot easier thanks to 512 wooden steps to the top.

From up there you can see an almost unchanged coastline. To the south is the roaring Southern Ocean pounding Pennington Bay and to the north the placid shallows of Pelican Lagoon, a natural bay which is now an aquatic reserve teeming with birdlife. Beyond that is Eastern Cove with the village of American River nestled on its protected western shore.

Other industries apart from sealing kept the area alive during later decades and a walking track through the native scrub on the shore of Eastern Cove leads to the ruins of an ambitious enterprise of the late 1800s. The Fish Cannery Walk explores what's left of a canning operation that processed snapper and King George whiting. Forty people were employed to prepare and cook the fish in cans.

But the cannery only survived a couple of years – the lack of refrigeration made it impossible to store big catches before processing. It's a well sign-posted walk among ruins and it reveals how determined the locals were to make a living.

Back towards Pelican Lagoon is what's left of Muston Wharf. In the early 1900s thousands of tonnes of salt mined from the island's lakes were loaded onto ships bound for the mainland. A fourteen-kilometre railway was built to the salt lake and a thriving township supported several hundred people by the water. It's all gone now and only a few forlorn concrete and wooden pylons are left of the wharf.

These days fishing and cruising charter boats are popular because the waters of American River are so protected. The island's oyster industry is booming and we saw a number of big oyster barges coming and going between the wharf and the long lines of posts that mark the leases.

The wharf is the place to be at four-thirty each afternoon when the local kiosk owner feeds the pelicans. It's a great opportunity to see these bizarre-looking birds jostle for an easy snack.

American River's guest houses invite you to spend time soaking up the heritage, fishing, wildlife and peacefulness of this quiet inlet. Pick up a local visitor guide from the Gateway Information Centre.

Penneshaw
South Australia 5222
Open Monday to Friday 9 am to 5 pm,
Saturday, Sunday and public holidays
10 am to 4 pm
Tel (08) 8553-1185
website www.tourkangarooisland.com.au
email tourki@kin.net.au

Gateway
Visitor
Information
Centre

Kangaroo Island Lighthouses
with Ron Kandelaars

Cape Willoughby Lighthouse

The Cape Willoughby Lighthouse stands proudly to attention on the eastern-most tip of Kangaroo Island. As we head towards it down a rough, scrub-lined dirt road, we begin to appreciate that the isolation of this wind-swept spot is as striking now as it was when the first keepers and their families came here more than 150 years ago. Their job was to operate the light and keep a constant watch over the treacherous waters between Cape Willoughby and the mainland – Backstairs Passage.

Work on building the lighthouse, the first in South Australia, began in 1849 with granite quarried from nearby hills. It was a slow process – workers would use a chisel and hammer to drill a hole, then they'd drive in a wooden plug, which they'd keep wet. The wood would absorb the moisture, expand and split the rock. So it's not surprising the lighthouse took three years to build.

The first keepers and their families came to Cape Willoughby more than 150 years ago   Photo by Adam Bruzzone

The original light has been replaced by an automatic signal   Photo by Adam Bruzzone

Three keepers and their families lived in the original cottages and, with monotonous regularity, they each made the lonely trek to the light to relieve one another at the end of eight-hour shifts. They say loneliness can drive a person mad, but for the keepers there were other hazards in their workplace.

The workings of the original light included a lens that weighed three tonnes. To reduce friction as it rotated, it floated in a bath of mercury. The keepers didn't know it at the time but they were probably being slowly poisoned as they breathed the fumes and absorbed the dangerous metal through their skin. The apparent madness of some of the keepers was probably due to mercury poisoning rather than loneliness. Now the mercury bath and revolving light have gone (the original light is on display at the Hope Cottage Museum at Kingscote) and so have the keepers. They've been replaced by an automatic signal.

There are three cottages named after the first keepers at Cape Willoughby, and they provide simple yet comfortable self-catered accommodation. The lighthouse is open for daily tours, as is the Weather and Interpretive Centre.

Willoughby Road via Penneshaw
South Australia 5222
Tel (08) 8553 1191
Accommodation bookings
(08) 8559 7235

Cape Willoughby
Lighthouse

Cape Borda Lighthouse

At the western end of Kangaroo Island, an unusual square shape on a 150-metre high clifftop can be seen for kilometres out to sea. The lighthouse at Cape Borda is a beacon to ships approaching the hazardous north-west coast but it is also a monument to extreme isolation and hardship. When first built in 1858, it was surely one of the most remote places in the world.

A landing at the foot of towering cliffs provided the only access to this part of the island. The only way in or out was by boat or by hacking your way through 100 kilometres of scrub and bush all the way to Kingscote. Some never left, like the first keeper, Captain Woodward. National Parks and Wildlife Ranger Dan Grieve read us a passage from Woodward's log:

'I tripped over a stump and fell and the stump pierced my right eye ... I fear I will lose sight in the eye – at 5.23 light winds moderate, west sou-west ...'

Dan says Woodward never mentions his injury again, concentrating instead on his weather observations. The meticulous log entries belied the nature of Woodward's injury and he died a few months later. Dan says the entry by the second keeper records Woodward's passing in the manner of all lightkeepers, with only relevant detail and no emotion:

'... at six winds moderate from the north-east, by noon winds freshening south to south west, Captain Woodward died.'

It's really when you go inside the lighthouse heritage museum and see photos of children and find their headstones in the nearby cemetery that you realise just how tough life here was. Thirteen people are buried in the cemetery including seven-year-old William

The cannon guarding against Russian invasion

Lighthouse cottages at Cape Borda

and three-year-old Arthur, the sons of Captain George Main. William died after another lightkeeper's children brought scarlet fever to the settlement and Arthur died after falling from a cliff.

The museum also reveals why this lighthouse was built on a lonely island at the bottom of the world. The clearing wasn't hacked out of the scrub and the lighthouse built just to warn ships about the rugged cliffs – Cape Borda's strategic position was recognised at a time when early colonial paranoia ran rife – many were convinced the Russians were coming.

A small cannon was sometimes used to signal ships of danger, but its primary use was to keep the Russians at bay. And, as Dan Grieve points out, it's done an excellent job!

Tours of the lighthouse and museum are conducted daily or you can settle into life as a keeper by checking into one of the cottages. Other cottages are available for hire at the Cape du Couedic lighthouse.

Flinders Chase National Park
Playford Highway
South Australia
Tel (08) 8559 3257
Accommodation bookings
(08) 8559 7235

Cape Borda
Lighthouse

Flinders Chase National Park
with Ron Kandelaars

Cape Barren Geese

There are few places in South Australia where you can still find big tracts of thick mallee scrub sweeping down to the coast, and Flinders Chase National Park is one of them. The mallee forms a dense wilderness covering the 32,000-hectare national park.

The park exists due to the efforts of early conservationists like Samuel Dixon, who spent much of his life battling various governments to save the western region of Kangaroo Island. The relentless search for new farming country had swallowed up much of the island by the late 1800s and governments didn't see the need for national parks back then. Dixon did, so he and others campaigned for nearly three decades until the park was finally declared in 1919.

In addition to being a wildlife haven, Dixon saw the park as essential to the preservation of human sanity. He described the area as a potential sanatorium and playground for tired workers suffering from what he quaintly described as 'brain fag'.

In many ways, Flinders Chase National Park has been an ongoing experiment ever since. Many threatened species were transported to the island from the mainland; most famously, in 1923, the koala. Their mainland habitat was under threat due to land

Wildlife up close

clearing and hunting so a number were relocated to Kangaroo Island where they took to the island's gum trees with relish. So much so that today their increasing numbers are presenting a new problem with many having to be shipped back to the mainland – a move that Samuel Dixon would probably have approved.

The koala is just one animal introduced from the mainland – Cape Barren geese, platypus and emus were also released and have since flourished alongside the kangaroos, wallabies, goannas and crimson rosellas native to the island's bush.

A visit to Flinders Chase National Park should include Rocky River where you're likely to catch a glimpse of the local koalas. If you're quiet and patient you might even see a platypus from the special viewing deck and walkway. Allow plenty of time to visit the new interpretive centre, which explains how Kangaroo Island and its wildlife have evolved through isolation.

Rocky River
South Australia
Tel (08) 8559 7235
website www.environment.sa.gov.au/
parks/kangaroo_is.html
Entry fee applies

Flinders Chase
Visitor Centre

Middle River Homestead
with Lisa McAskill

nelling Beach on Kangaroo Island's north coast is regarded as one of the island's top fishing spots. Locals and holiday-makers are often found wetting a line there just as old Henry Snelling did when he arrived from Adelaide with his wife and children in 1861. Before then sealers were known to camp on the banks of the nearby Middle River but there was no permanent settlement.

Postcards visited the area in the height of summer when the dry paddocks were proof of the importance of the river in opening up the north coast to settlement. We followed the river upstream into the surrounding hills and discovered a couple of cottages built on what is one of the oldest properties in the district – Middle River Homestead.

Middle River Beach   Photo by GK Ingram

The Bell family took up the land in the early 1900s and Ben Bell was soon quarrying the local limestone to build the family home. Like so much of the island, wool was essential to the growth of Middle River Homestead. The difficulty wasn't so much in herding the sheep within the natural contours of the gullies, but getting the wool clip to the markets in Adelaide. The roads were rough and the links with the mainland were unreliable.

The early settlers had to contend with loneliness and the likelihood that much-needed supplies might take weeks to arrive. Like most families who established small farms along the north coast, the Bells were hard-working, industrious people who tried to be as self-sufficient as possible by growing their own vegetables and meat, but during the lean times the bream that abound in Middle River must have been a tasty supplement to their diet. So too the sweet mulberries from the orchard they carved out of the scrub. These tough families also enjoyed their simple treats – a clearing they made for their weekend cricket matches stands as proof that life wasn't all work.

The plentiful wildlife, particularly kangaroos and tamar wallabies, makes Middle River Homestead a great location for a family holiday. But a word of advice: come nightfall the possums emerge and it's obvious that they've always had the run of the place.

The old Middle River Homestead and the two nearby cottages are available for hire and make a great north coast stop-over.

North coast of Kangaroo Island
Bookings thorugh Adventure Charters
of Kangaroo Island
Playford Highway, Cygnet River
South Australia 5223
Tel (08) 8553 9119
email wildlife@kin.net.au

Middle River
Homestead
and Cottages

The Remarkable Cape
with Lisa McAskill

ape du Couedic, on the south-western tip of Kangaroo Island, is a wild and remote place. It's home to one of the island's best-known landmarks, Remarkable Rocks. Like an oversize collection of rust-encrusted crockery the granite shapes perch on a dome jutting seventy-five metres over the sea. Their weather-sculptured shapes are the result of over 500 million years of erosion by the wind, rain and sea.

Remarkable Rocks, Kangaroo Island

Admiral's Arch is home to a colony of fur seals

Nearby is another of the Cape's landmarks, Admiral's Arch, a spectacular rock arch at the base of the cliffs that is home to a colony of New Zealand fur seals. Once endangered by hunting the seal population is now increasing by about thirty per cent a year.

The constant pounding of the surf is no threat to these characters. It usually offers a respite from the hustle and bustle of the colony as young males prepare themselves for the summer breeding season by staking out their territory. Fur seal pups can often be seen playing in pools under the Arch and are best seen from a viewing platform overlooking the colony.

Remarkable Rocks and Admiral's Arch are just two of the features of Flinders Chase National Park and are well worth the two-hour drive from the ferry terminal at Penneshaw.

Rocky River
South Australia
Tel (08) 8559 7235
website www.environment.sa.gov.au/
parks/kangaroo_is.html
Entry fee applies

Flinders Chase
Visitor Centre

River Murray

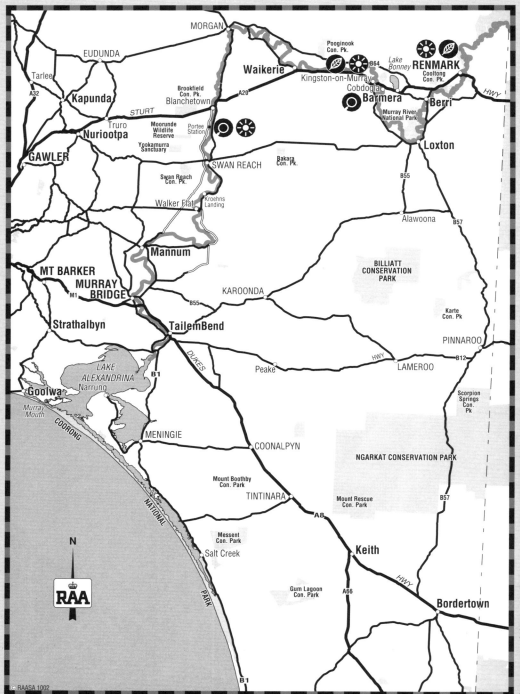

Food/Wine　　Walking/Activity　　History/Local Interest　　Nature/Wildlife

MORGAN

EUDUNDA

Tarlee

A32

Kapunda

STURT

Truro

Nuriootpa

GAWLER

Brookfield
Con. Pk.
Blanchetown

Moorunde
Wildlife
Reserve

Portee
Station

Ypokamurra
Sanctuary

SWAN REACH

Swan Reach
Con. Pk.

Walker Flat

Kroehns
Landing

Mannum

MT BARKER

MURRAY
BRIDGE

M1

Strathalbyn

TailemBend

DUKES

B55

Goolwa

Murray
Mouth

COORONG

NATIONAL

N

RAA

PARK

LAKE
ALEXANDRINA
Narrung

B1

MENINGIE

Peake

Mount Boothby
Con. Park

TINTINARA

Messent
Con. Park

Salt Creek

Gum Lagoon
Con. Park

Waikerie

A20

Pooginook
Con. Pk.

Kingston-on-Murray

B64

Cobdogla

Barmera

Lake
Bonney

RENMARK

Cooltong
Con. Pk.

Berri

HWY

Murray River
National Park

Loxton

B55

Bakara
Con. Pk.

KAROONDA

B55

Alawoona

B57

BILLIATT
CONSERVATION
PARK

Karte
Con. Pk

PINNAROO

HWY

LAMEROO

B12

Scorpion
Springs
Con.
Pk

COONALPYN

NGARKAT CONSERVATION PARK

Mount Rescue
Con. Park

B57

A8

Keith

A66

HWY

Bordertown

© RAASA 1002

Reverse: Eucalyptus tree on the banks of the River Murray

South Australians have an intimate relationship with the River Murray. It is one of our most important lifelines – often providing up to 90 per cent of our metropolitan water supply. But the Murray does more than just quench our thirst – it is one of our favourite year-round playgrounds. As one river fanatic put it, 'Once you've drunk the water, that's it – you'll always love the river!'

Whether you spend an afternoon picnicking on its banks or a week cruising its bends on a houseboat, it's easy to get hooked. The mighty Murray offers so much – the towering red sandstone cliffs are a classic postcard image, so too are the shore-hugging orchards and vineyards and ancient river red gums.

Our River Murray experience ends as the river itself does – in the magnificent waters of Lake Alexandrina. Sadly, the beauty of the lake masks the creeping salinity and limited flow problems that threaten the river's future. We all need to do our bit by not contributing to these already considerable problems.

What You'll Find in this Region

- A visit to Portee Station is a classic River Murray experience that draws together many facets of river life.
- We appreciate the extremes of the Murray on a Loch Luna Voyage that reveals the river's creeks and backwaters that hold their own secrets.
- Next stop is Cobdogla Irrigation Museum where we'll meet Big Thumper, the irrigation pump with personality.
- Relaxing on a houseboat isn't the only way of enjoying the river – waterskiing is a popular sport on the river's smooth waters.

Tips From the Crew

- If you're looking for a great view in a pub setting, Ron recommends the Pretoria Hotel at Mannum.

- Lisa says the Mallee Fowl Restaurant near Monash is a real treat for lovers of good food and country music.

- Keith recommends a stroll around the boardwalks at Banrock Station. He says you'll discover wonderful birdlife in a tranquil wetland setting.

River Murray near Akuna Station   Photo by Keith Conlon

Want More Information?

SA Visitor and Travel Centre
1300 655 276

Riverland Hotline
1300 657 625

Riverland website
www.riverland.info

Mannum Visitor Information Centre
(08) 8569 1303

National Parks and Wildlife SA
(08) 8576 3690

RAA Touring (maps and guides)
(08) 8202 4600

SA Tourism Commission website
www.southaustralia.com

***Postcards* website**
www.postcards.sa.com

I Didn't Know That!

• Renmark was originally called Bookmark and is the oldest irrigation settlement in Australia.

• The River Murray was first discovered in 1824 by explorers Hume and Hovell near Albury in New South Wales. They called it the Hume but Captain Charles Sturt later named it the Murray during his 77-day trip down the river in 1830.

• The Aboriginal meaning of Waikerie is 'many wings'. Coincidentally, Waikerie is a world-renowned spot for gliding.

• After World War I, the Soldier Settlement Scheme provided returned soldiers with farming land at Barmera, Berri, Cadell, Renmark, Winkie, Glossop and Waikerie.

Portee Station
with Keith Conlon

Portee Station Homestead   Photo courtesy Ian Clark

P ortee Station is only two hours' drive from Adelaide and a visit lets you see a working sheep station and get a taste of the outback. It also has strong links with one of the men responsible for opening up this country.

Portee Station is about ten kilometres south of Blanchetown and is owned by Ian and Margaret Clark who balance the demands of station work with outback hospitality. The sign and windsock near the station entrance amused the *Postcards* crew, it read 'Portee International Airport', and we chuckled, but it turned out to be close to the truth. As Ian explained, about two-thirds of his guests are international visitors, and many of them arrive by charter plane.

Two-thirds of Portee's guests are international visitors   Photo courtesy Ian Clark

Portee's centre-piece is a magnificently restored homestead surrounded by expansive lawns that sweep down from the front door to Portee Creek. There's a huge billabong lined with majestic river red gums, and the unmistakable coloured clay cliffs of the Murray River are visible about a kilometre away across the flood plains of the mighty river.

For me the highlight of the trip was a visit to the site of explorer Edward John Eyre's home on a part of Portee called Moorunde, a place with a certain eeriness about it. While nothing of the house, courthouse or police barracks remain, the long avenue of gums referred to in Eyre's journals still stand – proudly marking the place where he exercised great influence.

Eyre's reputation as an explorer was matched by his enlightened approach to Aboriginal issues in the fledgling colony. As a young overlander bringing sheep to Adelaide via the Murray in 1839, he encountered Moorunde Creek and saw his future. He took up his land grant here, which became one of the first settlements outside Adelaide, in 1841, after his epic Nullabor crossing.

It wasn't long before he was appointed magistrate and Protector of Aborigines in the region. His task was a difficult one as frequent clashes between river Aboriginal tribes and overlanders had left fifty Aborigines dead and thousands of sheep missing. Eyre successfully promoted peace in the area and, according to his friend Captain Charles Sturt, he was a 'guardian hero'.

During his time at Moorunde, Eyre experimented with irrigation and grew crops and vegetables but regular floods eventually led to the abandonment of the site in favour of Blanchetown upstream.

In contrast to the dry-looking paddocks and yards, a boat trip at dusk along Portee Creek is a bird-watcher's dream. The long billabong begins from the Big Lagoon, where pelicans preen themselves in the fading light. As dark crept over the flats, our return trip was memorable for the screeching sulphur-crested cockatoos and little corellas as they swept over the water.

Chowilla woolshed   Photo by Keith Conlon

All the history and station touring are good for the appetite and, as we wandered back to the homestead, Ian's daughter Susan was basting a butterfly-boned leg of lamb on the barbecue with her secret Portee marinade. A station dinner with more time for bush yarns was exactly what we needed to round off a truly Australian experience.

Blanchetown
South Australia 5357
Tel (08) 8540 5211
email ian@portee.com.au
website www.portee.com.au

Portee
Station

Loch Luna Voyages
with Ron Kandelaars

I f you are ever lucky enough to fly over the Murray River you'll realise just how complex the ancient river system is. From the air the anabranches of the main river fan out like capillaries, and from the bow of Peter Foley's MV *Loch Luna* you get a closer view of the importance of these channels and wetlands.

The Murray is a complex ancient river system

We left Kingston-on-Murray bound for the backwaters that lead into Lake Bonney and it wasn't long before we were in the wetlands known as Loch Luna. We passed an obvious line of dead gum trees which Peter told us marks the old Nockburra Creek. Like so much else around here it is now under water thanks to the nearby lock built in 1925. The shallow water in these parts means only the adventurous in canoes or shallow draft boats can venture in, creating a peaceful haven for birds.

Peter pointed out the many tree stumps – reminders of the impact of the cross-saw in the early days of the riverboat trade. Timber cutters and their families were dotted along the bank every forty kilometres or so and they'd pile wood on the bank. They were the service stations for the paddle steamers which used to burn about a ton of wood every three hours. As Peter said, we should be thankful the timber cutters didn't have chainsaws otherwise there wouldn't be any trees left at all.

We pushed on into the narrow waters of Chambers Creek, named after John Chambers who took up a pastoral lease on Cobdogla Station in 1846. He didn't spend

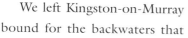

Aborigines carved canoes from gum trees on the Murray

The MV *Loch Luna* lands at Chambers Creek

Photo by Pete Foley

much time here though his grand home overlooking the city from Montefiore Hill in North Adelaide gives you some idea of the wealth generated by pastoral holdings like Cobdogla. Chambers sponsored John McDouall Stuart's exploration of inland Australia.

As the MV *Loch Luna* cuts her way through the thick duck weed which helps oxygenate the still waters of Chambers Creek we sight a local landmark – Sugarloaf Hill.

Peter explained that the sandstone outcrop was important to the original inhabitants of the area, the Barmedki people. From the top they had a great view of the flood plain and beyond. When Charles Sturt came through in 1830 he wrote in his journal about a big column of smoke coming from the hill – obviously a warning to those downstream that Sturt's party was on its way.

Sturt's arrival would change the lives of the Barmedki forever. His glowing reports of arable land further south prompted authorities in London to press ahead with a new colony called South Australia.

The story of Sturt's journey through this part of the Murray is just one of many that comes to life as part of Peter Foley's three-hour Loch Luna voyage.

Kingston-On-Murray
South Australia 5331
Bookings (08) 8583 0223
email thepines@sa.ozland.net.au
website www.murray-river.net

Loch Luna
Eco Cruises

Cobdogla Irrigation and Steam Museum
with Ron Kandelaars

These days the Loveday Flyer's job is to take visitors on a trip around the Cobdogla Irrigation and Steam Museum, but the Flyer holds a far more significant position in the history of this part of the Riverland. In 1921 she was one of two 24-gauge locomotives used to build the area's massive irrigation system.

Cobdogla is on the Murray near Barmera and, in the early 1900s, it was decided that the success of the orchard industry further upstream could be duplicated in the area between Cobdogla and Berri. Workers shifted mountains of sand and rock, dug trenches and built open channels and pipelines and, by 1922, the job was finished and a flood of soldier settlers arrived on the promise of well-irrigated land.

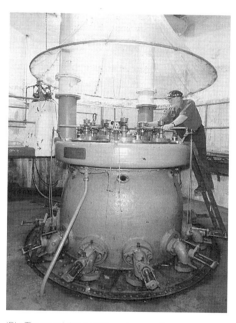

'Big Thumper' the world's only operating Humphrey Pump.

The Cobdogla Irrigation and Steam Museum is a living tribute to those early years. Big Thumper, the world's only operating Humphrey pump, has been faithfully restored and makes a big impact when working. Named after its English designer, Herbert Alfred Humphrey, Big Thumper is a four-stroke gas-powered pump that acts like a giant water cannon propelling as much as 220 tons of water with each stroke. It's capable of pumping more than one million gallons of water an hour and played a big part in the early irrigation of the surrounding orchards.

The Loveday Flyer

There are plenty other ground-shaking machines at Cobdogla, like the massive Fowler Traction Engine. Built in England in the early 1920s it was one of six driven down from Port Augusta to work on the irrigation scheme. Its restoration is another example of the work of the Cobdogla Steam Friends Society. The museum also has an impressive history of the area run by the National Trust.

Park Terrace, Cobdogla
South Australia 5346
For operating days contact the
Barmera Visitor Information Centre
Barwell Avenue, Barmera
South Australia 5345
Tel (08) 8588 2289
Weekend inquiries
(08) 8588 7031

Cobdogla
Irrigation and
Steam Museum

Waterskiing at Renmark
with Lisa McAskill

On a hot autumn day at Renmark in the Riverland, it's time for me to overcome all my fears of high-octane water sports. And while I have a bit of trouble getting my skis on, it's not long, under Barton William's expert guidance, before I'm in the river hanging onto a boom pole, with Barton only a couple of arm-lengths away in the back of the boat. He wears a headset and talks to me through a loud speaker, so I can hang onto his words of encouragement while I'm finding my river feet!

Lisa tests her skills   Photo by Jeff Clayfield

Look at that ... you're a natural. Stay low. Good. I want you to slowly use your legs. Just push up with your legs. Slowly. Okay, well done!

As the boat gently pulls me along, I follow Barton's instructions.

Good. Let your arms go straight. Right. Straighten your back. Now push with your back straight. Whoa. Alright, now let go! Well done.

With Jackie Crofton at the wheel of the boat this husband and wife team can examine your skiing style at close quarters, all the while providing the confidence that they bring to high-level competition. Barton is the state and national Barefoot Waterski Champion and, as he says, confidence is important, but pride tends to come before a fall.

As I start to gain some confidence, he tells me to slowly look to the horizon and lift my head. His next bit of advice is put rather elegantly:

Avoid pulling with your arms or your bum will travel over the water a lot faster than the rest of you!

Waterskiing is suitable for most ages and, like any sport, it's perseverance that pays off in the long run. Barton and Jackie teach a range of students with a tried and true combination of encouragement, experience and the right equipment:

Our youngest student is a four-year-old from Adelaide and he's a regular. Our eldest is in his late fifties. So anyone, regardless of age, can do it with the equipment we've got. The correct type of skis, the boom bar and the head set, and the progressive stages that we go through with correct warm up and technique.

Under Barton and Jackie's tuition you may soon gravitate from twin skis to wave and kneeboards and, eventually, to no boards at all. Barefoot skiing was the inspiration for the school's name 'Footing Fever' and Barton says it sums up that special feeling when the skier and the water almost become one.

If you'd like to have a go at waterskiing on the scenic River Murray, give Barton or Jackie a call.

Contact Barton Williams
and Jackie Crofton
Tel 0419 500 652
Lessons start at $35 hour

Footing
Fever

Wakefield Press and Channel Nine thank the following organisations and individuals for use of their photos in *Postcards: On the road again.*

Gill Albers, p 126; Australian Arid Lands Botanic Garden, p 57, 58; Botanic Gardens of Adelaide, p 29, 30, 32; Bridgewater Mill, p 23, 24; Allan Childs, p 87; Ian Clark, p 171, 172; Cleland Wildlife Park, p 25, 26; Cobdogla Irrigation Museum, p 177, 178; Coorong Cruises, p 50; Department for Environment and Heritage, p 52, 157, 158, 159, 160, 161; Granite Island Nature Park, p 44; Robyn Hill, p 128; Melrose Districts Historical Society, p 59; Nangare Design, p 22; Ian Roberts, p 123; SA Tourism, p 48, 69, 71, 119, 162, 165, 166; South Australian Company Store, p 138, 143, 144; Strathalbyn National Trust Museum, p 33; Tanunda Kegel Club, p 141; Tourism Eyre Peninsula, p 101, 103, 106, 108, 110, 111, 113, 116, 118; Yalumba Winery, p 148, 149, 150